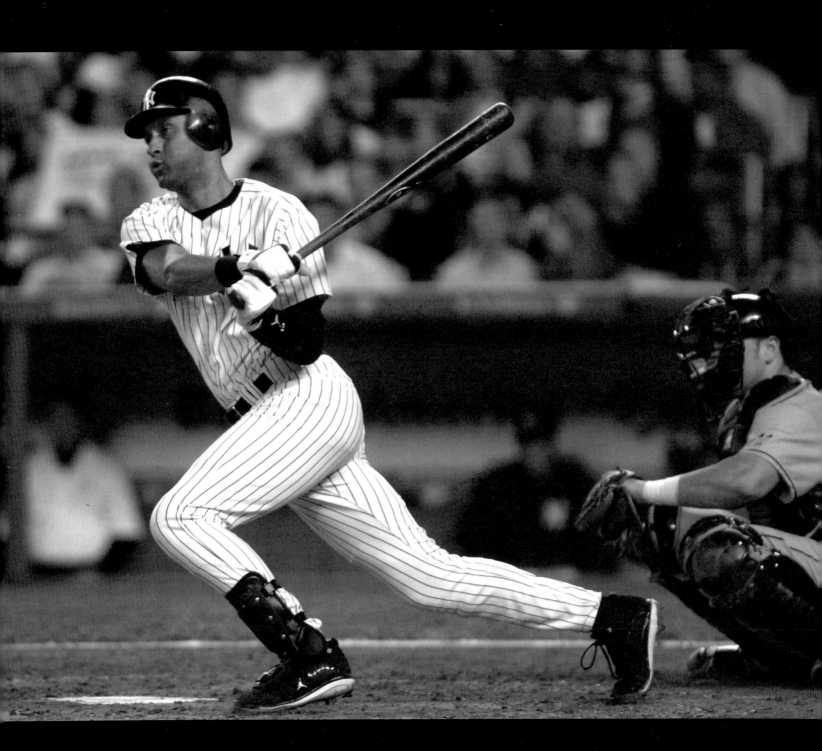

"I've used the same bat—same model, same size—
since day one in the minor leagues."
— DEREK JETER, NEW YORK YANKEES SHORTSTOP AND NINE-TIME ALL-STAR

CONTENTS

Foreword

BY KEN GRIFFEY JR.

Sports, and the desire to be part of a winning team, have always been important in my family. My grandfather played baseball in high school, where he was a teammate of Stan Musial. My grandmother played basketball in high school, and my mother was a volleyball player. I played football at Cincinnati's Moeller High School and was fortunate to be part of an Ohio state championship team my junior year. But my senior year in high school, I stopped playing football to focus on my true love of all the sports—baseball.

Growing up in the shadow of Major League Baseball during my father's 19-year playing career, I had the unique opportunity to learn the game from the inside out. When my dad, Ken Griffey Sr., starred as an outfielder for Cincinnati during the Big Red Machine's two World Series wins in the 1970s, I was barely in grade school, but I was getting an education whether I knew it or not.

My father brought me into the clubhouse on a regular basis, and I learned firsthand about baseball's unique competition and time-tested tradition. Looking back, some might wonder why he let me hang around the ballpark so much at such a young age. I ran around the place with Pete Rose Jr. and Tony Perez's boys, Eddie and Victor, and we played games of pickle, where we threw the ball back and forth, trying to get the runner out.

My father knew how much it meant to me, being around both him and the big-league game. I always wanted to wear his cap, even though it was too big. I would flip it around backward so I could see. Anything I could do to get closer to him and closer to baseball. It was always that way, I'm told. My parents say I started carrying around an oversized plastic baseball bat about the same time I started walking. I never wanted to put it down.

By the time I was 11, I was having what should have been considered a pretty good season in the youth league. Nobody got me out until the end of the year, but when they did, I cried so hard my coach had to take me out of the game. Often when my father had a day off and came to watch me play in high school, I struggled at the plate, trying a little bit too hard. The next time at bat, though, I was confident I could hit the ball out of the park. That's the thing about baseball. It's a game of possibilities against the most challenging odds. The possibilities keep us coming back for more.

After my junior year of football, I felt I needed to concentrate on just one sport. In football, I was a running back, and my father advised me that I could play a little longer in baseball than football. Even though I enjoyed my time as a running back in high school, I didn't care all that much for getting hit. So that was it. Baseball would be the sport I would concentrate on. The next year, 1987, I was drafted in the first round by the Seattle Mariners, and I remember thinking I wanted to get to the big leagues within about 15 minutes.

It did not happen that quickly, but when the Mariners put me in the lineup in 1989, my father was still playing as a professional. The next year, we would take the field together. As I look back over the years of my own career, the first time we played on the same field, wearing the same uniform, is a highlight.

The date was August 31, 1990. My father had just been signed by the Mariners, and we were both penciled in the lineup, batting back-to-back. My father's first time up, he got a hit. My first time up, I got a hit, too. The very next month, we had back-to-back home runs in a game. That had never happened before in Major League Baseball, a father and son playing at the same time, and the experience is something I will never forget.

The experience was fitting since through him I observed the dedication and practice it takes to become successful. He worked with me constantly, and we always tried new things. He believed that the game was 90 percent mental and only 10 percent physical, but that didn't keep him from trying to find the perfect equipment. We tried different shoes. We tested all sorts of gloves. We even tested a few bats, but we quickly settled on the Louisville Slugger, and that became one piece of equipment we never changed again.

The link we experienced, beginning with my father's playing days in the early 1970s and continuing four decades later, is similar to the link many players and fans alike have to baseball. The game changes over the years. Players run faster. Balls are hit harder. New ballparks are built. But the one thing that does not change is baseball's connection to the past, and for many of us that starts with Louisville Slugger, the bat that has been a part of the game for 125 years.

I was in my first year with Seattle when I signed on to put my name on a Louisville Slugger. About the only thing my father and I ever disagreed on relating to bats was which model Louisville Slugger was the best. He wanted me to use the S216 like he did, but I prefer the C271 with its smaller barrel. At 34 inches long and 31 ounces, it is one of the smallest bats used in the big leagues, but I always liked the speed I can get with it.

Over the years I have been able to get to know the people at Hillerich & Bradsby Co., makers of Louisville Slugger. Professional player representative Chuck Schupp was the first one I knew well. He's the one who came to Seattle to visit with me and talk about what it meant to become one of a long line of guys who had autographed bat agreements. My dad and I have visited the factory a few times and met the Hillerich family. I found that these are people who genuinely love the game. They love players and want to support them. They want to know what they can do to make bats that give a player the confidence to be his or her best. They want to be a part of history, and they understand that history can't be separated from the game itself.

Baseball and the Louisville Slugger bats have grown up together. When you see that wall in the museum that has thousands of player signatures on it, all the way back to Babe Ruth and Ted Williams and Jackie Robinson and all those guys that really made the game bigger than life, you understand how Louisville Slugger has been a part of the game since the beginning. That's why I am pleased to be a part of this book, looking back over 125 years of baseball history. It's a great reminder that the links that run throughout the history of the sport are what keep baseball a great game.

Ken Griffey Jr.
Recipient of the Louisville Slugger Museum & Factory
Living Legend Award in 2007

"There's a history to Louisville Slugger that
I think everyone in baseball respects."

—JIM THOME, CHICAGO WHITE SOX DH AND 14TH ON MAJOR LEAGUE BASEBALL'S ALL-TIME
HOME-RUN LIST

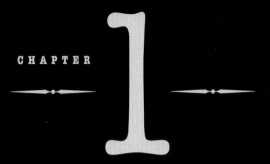

Crafting Baseball's Bat

Baseball would be an entirely different and decidedly less significant game without its time-tested traditions, legends, and lore. Imagine the Yankees without pinstripes on their uniforms or the legacy of legendary slugger Babe Ruth. Envision a day at Fenway Park without the Green Monster or a trip to Wrigley Field without the seventh-inning stretch. Consider how former Boston Red Sox great Carl Yastrzemski might have performed in his prime had he not worn the same pair of red socks game after game from 1967 to 1973.

And wonder how Ruth—America's first home-run sultan—and Yastrzemski—the last man to win the coveted Triple Crown—might have fared at the plate without their customized Louisville Slugger bats.

Louisville Slugger did not, of course, invent either the game of baseball or the baseball bat itself. But since the late 1800s, the family-owned company has made what is arguably baseball's signature product—the Louisville Slugger bat—and continues to play a significant role in the evolution of America's pastime. For the past 125 years, Louisville Slugger has crafted millions of bats in a myriad of shapes and sizes for both amateur and professional players.

More than just a contest played by an ever-changing cast of players in the field, baseball is a quilt—a patchwork of feats, failures, and features of today directly and uniquely tied to those of yesterday.

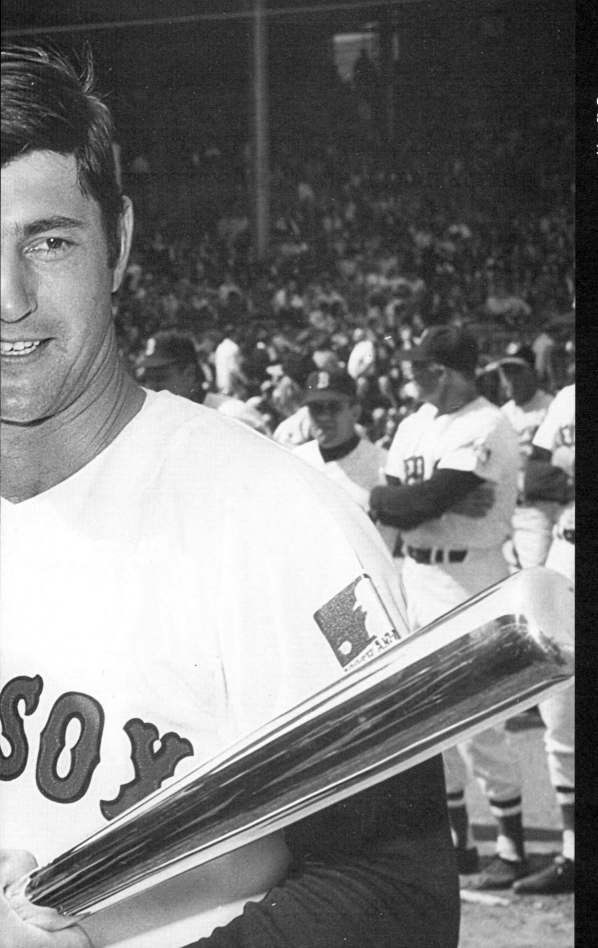

Carl Yastrzemski won the Silver Bat Award in 1963, 1967, and 1968 with the Boston Red Sox.

1833

J. FREDERICH
HILLERICH IS BORN
IN GERMANY

In 1914, 19-year-old George Herman Ruth Jr.'s enormous talent caught the eye of Jack Dunn, owner and manager of the Baltimore Orioles (then a minor league team). When the players called him "Jack's newest babe," the name stuck, and George Jr. will forever be known as "Babe."

1842

THE FAMILY OF J.
MICHAEL HILLERICH,
J. FREDERICH'S
FATHER, EMIGRATES
TO AMERICA AND
SOON FINDS ITS
WAY TO LOUISVILLE,
KENTUCKY

Babe Ruth, for example, custom-ordered his bats from Louisville Slugger. The man once considered the undisputed best hitter in baseball hit all of his then-record 60 home runs in 1927 with the Louisville Slugger model R43. He made subtle changes to the bat during his career before retiring in 1935, routinely ordering modifications including varying the length of his bats from 36 to 37 inches and their weight from 36 to 47 ounces (though the heaviest weight was only used in spring training).

Decades after Ruth retired, players have continued swinging the Louisville Slugger R43, making it one of Louisville Slugger's 10 most popular models. Legendary Cincinnati Reds catcher Johnny Bench preferred the Ruth-inspired R43. So did Hall of Fame and Philadelphia Phillies third baseman Mike Schmidt, who is said to have hit home run No. 500 with an R43.

That Schmidt sought power and inspiration from the same model and brand of bat that Ruth swung is more remarkable because the Philadelphia slugger was actually under contract to another bat manufacturer—Adirondack—and not Louisville Slugger. But since he often preferred taking a Louisville Slugger to the plate, Schmidt devised a way to keep his sponsor happy—he was known to place a ring of red tape around the middle of the bat to mimic on television the look of the Adirondack, known for the colored ring around its middle.

Such stories—from the intricate customization of a bat to the link between two great hitters separated by five decades—help weave the timeless game of baseball into our national fabric.

"We did not build a model and give it to
the player to use.
The player told us what
he wanted and we built it."
— John A. "Jack" Hillerich III

ORIGINS OF THE GAME

The relationship between baseball and the bat did not start out quite that romantically, however. In the early 1800s, versions of what would become the modern game of baseball were being played around the United States, but the bats used were more crude tools than cultural icons. Players in the field did not have gloves, and the game itself had little refinement and few consistent rules. In short, the tradition and historical eloquence that enthusiasts recognize today was not part of the game at its start.

In Philadelphia, for example, players in the late 18th and early 19th century played a raw version of baseball known as "town ball." The contest typically included more than nine players on a field that had no foul lines. Bats came in all shapes and sizes, depending on the player's choice. Some were square, others were skinny like a broomstick, and most players made their own. By the mid-19th century in New York, however, the evolution of the game was underway and baseball's culture of tradition was in its formative stage.

The official birth of American baseball occurred in 1845 when a 25-year-old New Yorker named Alexander Cartwright combined what he saw as the best of various baseball guidelines with some tweaks of his own and published the rules of baseball for his New York Knickerbocker Club. Closely resembling those that govern today's game, Cartwright's rules—which called for nine players per team and clearly defined a field of play—were quickly adopted outside of New York, giving the game much-needed uniformity. The formalization led to a recorded game between the Knickerbockers and the New York Baseball Club in Hoboken, New Jersey, in 1846 as the first seeds of tradition were planted. Baseball's new guidelines created captivating contests, effectively blending human athleticism with board-game strategy.

As the basic framework of the game developed, its popularity rapidly rose in America. With the Civil War over and the Industrial Revolution and its economic boom beginning, the game was positioned to become the nation's preferred sport for players and spectators both. The Cincinnati Red Stockings became baseball's first openly all-professional team in 1869 (though the team only lasted for one more year before disbanding amid bankruptcy).

Along with baseball's rules refinements were regulations adopted in 1869 that bats could be no

J. Frederich Hillerich, founder of J.F. Hillerich Job Turning

1845

ALEXANDER
CARTWRIGHT
PUBLISHES HIS
RULES OF BASEBALL
FOR THE NEW YORK
KNICKERBOCKER
CLUB, TAKING
THE FIRST MAJOR
STEP TOWARD
THE CREATION OF
MODERN BASEBALL

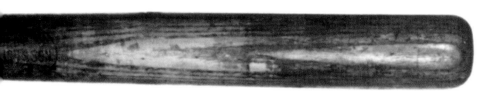

Bats have undergone slight changes over the years, but the basic bat first turned in 1884 would still be recognized by baseball fans today.

longer than 42 inches—the same size limitation still in force today—but players still used them in many different shapes and sizes. Some players used square bats for bunting, while others played with square-handled bats. Others preferred thick handles, resulting in a bat that was nearly uniform in width from handle to barrel. Players selected their bat of choice often based on little more than a hunch; if they happened to connect solidly in a game with one, they often used that one bat until someone convinced them otherwise. The bat, in other words, was still evolving by trial and error.

In 1871, the National Association of Professional Base Ball Players was formed, creating a league of nine competing teams. Even though bats were still rudimentary and came in all shapes and sizes, the ball had become harder and was causing fielders—especially pitchers, because of their proximity to the plate—to suffer increasingly bruised hands after games. One of baseball's most prominent pitchers in the 1870s—who later become a renowned name in the sporting goods business—recalled the first time he saw a glove on a player's hand during a game. Worn by first baseman Charles C. Waitt of St. Louis in 1875, the glove was flesh-colored and featured a round opening in the back.

"I asked Waitt about his glove," recalled A.G. Spalding in 1911. "He confessed that he was a bit ashamed to wear it but had it on to save his hand. He also admitted that he had chosen a color as inconspicuous as possible, because he didn't care to attract attention."

Two years after seeing Waitt's glove, Spalding began to use one himself, adding padding until the sting from catching the ball finally eased on his hand. Although gloves were not mandatory until the mid-1880s, most players were already using them and had considerably advanced fielding accuracy. As a result, the batter needed to counter the improved defense with more ability at the plate. This was easier said than done, though, because nobody really knew how best to craft a piece of lumber that would most effectively strike a pitched ball.

Baseball as a sport, however, had matured considerably since its early, disorganized birth, and many Americans easily took to the sport. A piece of wood, a crude glove, and loose-fitting uniforms donned after a long day in the factory or field transformed America's working class into passionate and able ballplayers. Such was the state of America at a time when man was merely limited by ambition. He could overcome limitations of birthright and position to find wealth and stardom through talent, work ethic, and the strength of his own conviction. America, after all, had become a nation of mobility.

Travel by steam-powered trains and boats had transformed arduous, long-distance journeys into commonplace trips available to many. The reality of affordable travel had burned itself into the developing American mind-set, making road trips for baseball teams an attainable goal. Also, the use of instant information transfer via telegraph helped baseball emerge as a national game; journalists could report results and rivalries from city to city quickly and cheaply.

Away from the ballfield, the American worker was prospering. At an 1884 labor convention in Chicago, the eight-hour workday—long sought by organized labor to reduce a work day that was sometimes as long as 16 hours—was officially declared as the goal for American businesses and manufacturers to reach within two years. This new standard would provide, as one advocate described it, equal time in the day for work, rest, and play. Play became a critical interest of Americans who had already established their willingness to work hard. A century earlier, the founding fathers had declared that all people were endowed with rights that included "the pursuit of Happiness," and many Americans were pursuing this happiness through their newfound enthusiasm for sports.

Baseball emerged as more than a sport; it reflected the mood of the nation. The game engendered personal and civic pride, represented proof of America's success in easing the burden of a working-class citizenry, and symbolized the equality of opportunity. A new social standard was forming in which play and sport would emerge as important, worthy pursuits, and no sport captured the attention of players and spectators like baseball.

Professional teams sprouted in three leagues from Wilmington, North Carolina (Wilmington Quicksteps of the Union Association), to Toledo, Ohio (Toledo Blue Stockings of the American Association), to Providence, Rhode Island (Providence Grays of the National League). Likewise, favorite players emerged as some of the country's first sporting heroes, and perhaps no player stood out more than Pete Browning, who played in 1884 for the Louisville Eclipse of Louisville, Kentucky (the franchise, a member of the American Association, changed its name to the Louisville Colonels in 1885).

CUSTOM MADE

Often referred to as the "southernmost northern city" because it sits along the Ohio River in north-central Kentucky just south of the Indiana border, Louisville was in the 1880s as it is today, a municipality at a cultural crossroads. With blended qualities of the Midwest and the Deep South, the city had from its earliest days an ambitious spirit marked by most river towns at the turn of the century. On Louisville's west side, Pete Browning's family ran a prosperous grocery until his father, Samuel Browning, was killed by a cyclone in 1874.

The youngest of the Brownings' eight children, Pete was just 13 years old when his father died, and it was apparent he could not follow his father as a successful proprietor. Browning suffered from mastoiditis, an inner-ear affliction that made him virtually deaf. Embarrassed that he could not hear, Browning avoided school and was essentially illiterate.

Where Browning excelled was in athletics or games of almost any type. An accomplished marbles player, as a teenager he had to travel to Louisville's east side to find a game because he had swept marbles from all his friends and peers on the west side. He was also an accomplished skater—"easily the best in Louisville"—but it was on the baseball diamond where he truly found his fame. Browning began playing for the Louisville Eclipse in 1877 at the age of 16 and within four months had pitched a shutout win against a National League team, the Louisville Grays.

But Browning's biggest contributions came at the plate, not from on the mound or in the field. In fact, many observers felt he could barely field

The Louisville Eclipse first fielded an American Association team in 1882 and were the forerunners of the Louisville Colonels (1885–1899).

at all; Browning was known to bungle routine fly balls and botch grounders.

Alcohol abuse plagued Browning beginning in his teenage years, continuing throughout his career, and lasting until the day he died. He was single and lived alone with his mother, but that did not stop Browning from drinking. As early as 1882, he was chided in print by a Louisville journalist for playing a game inebriated, and he

openly admitted that he could not hit the ball as a batter until he hit the bottle.

But oh, could he hit the ball. Few major league players could come close to hitting the baseball like Pete Browning did. He led the league in batting in his first season (a .378 average) and was among baseball's top hitters every year he played until he retired in the early 1890s. As a hitter, he had a flair that other players did not possess. Known to name his bats after biblical figures, he was said to have always been on the prowl for a new "magical" stick. Browning's quest for a bat containing more potential hits apparently led to a relationship with a teenaged Louisville woodworker who could grant his wish.

John A. "Bud" Hillerich was just 17 years old when Pete Browning was slugging baseballs for the Louisville Eclipse professional baseball team in 1884. The son of German immigrant J. Frederich Hillerich and Ella (Ward) Hillerich, Bud worked in his family's woodworking shop, opened in Louisville in 1859, as an apprentice. The shop, eventually located on downtown Louisville's Clay Street and named J.F. Hillerich Job Turning, was known for custom-carving wood for everything from bedposts to chairs, railings, and butter churns.

Using lathes—machinery that turns wood on an axis while a sharp chisel cuts or scrapes it into a desired shape—the Hillerich family served America's expanding need and desire for furnishings during the country's robust growth period in the latter half of the 19th century. And it just so happened that for young Bud Hillerich, himself a passionate amateur baseball player, the lathe was also the preferred tool for crafting baseball bats.

Hillerich, according to his grandson Jack Hillerich, was a bit of a black sheep in the family, in part because he loved baseball, and the sport in the late 1880s was still viewed by some Americans as the working-class man's excuse for skipping an afternoon of labor. In fact, on the day Louisville Slugger is said to have been invented, young Bud Hillerich was not in his father's woodworking

Despite a severe hearing problem, Pete Browning is considered by many to be the greatest hitter not in the National Baseball Hall of Fame. He was a three-time batting champion and retired with a .341 lifetime average.

shop but out at the ballfield, watching his beloved Louisville Eclipse play an afternoon game at Eclipse Park, located at 28th and Elliott Streets in the city's west end.

Legend has it that as Hillerich watched his heroes from the stands, Pete Browning broke his favorite bat. After the game, the woodworking apprentice approached Browning and offered to make a new, customized bat for the slugger down at the family shop. Browning obliged, and after making a trip to J.F. Hillerich Job Turning, he emerged with a new bat cut and trimmed from a piece of white ash—a tree that grows in New York and Pennsylvania and is known for its strength, resiliency, and weight, key ingredients for any baseball bat. The next day, the baseball player nicknamed the "Louisville Slugger" for his

1859
J. MICHAEL'S SON J. FREDERICH HILLERICH OPENS A "JOB TURNING" BUSINESS, LEARNED FROM HIS FATHER, IN LOUISVILLE TO MAKE SUCH ITEMS AS BEDPOSTS, HAND RAILS, AND BOWLING PINS

1866
J. FREDERICH'S SON, JOHN ANDREW "BUD" HILLERICH, IS BORN

11

Bats, bedposts, a swinging butter churn, and other products of the Hillerich woodworking shop are displayed in this photo believed to have been taken in 1889. Included are both founder J. Frederich (second from left in his characteristic long beard) and his son Bud (on the right in the doorway). The prominence of bats confirms the photo was taken well after the first bat was made in 1884.

1871

THE NATIONAL
ASSOCIATION OF
PROFESSIONAL BASE
BALL PLAYERS IS
FORMED, CREATING
A LEAGUE OF NINE
TEAMS

Browning's eccentricities—including his tendency to catch fly balls standing on one leg, his refusal to slide, and his belief that staring into the sun improved his eyesight—leave us with many stories and much lore.

prodigious production at the plate proceeded to get three hits.

By 1885, Browning had won another batting title, and word spread throughout baseball about his Hillerich-made bats. Years later, in 1914, Bud Hillerich confirmed in a newspaper interview that he was involved with the creation of Browning's bat, though suggesting that he only "carved a ring" in the Louisville Slugger's weapon to give the superstitious player good luck.

DIVERGENT POSSIBILITIES

More than 125 years after Browning is said to have taken his famed first cuts at the plate, descendants

of Bud Hillerich and archivists at the family-owned company that still produces Louisville Slugger bats have resisted confirming the exact version of the story because they believe their bats help players make history, not the other way around.

Some historians argue the first bat made by the Hillerich family was given to a third baseman for the St. Louis Browns named Arlie Latham in 1883 or 1884. During an interview published in 1937 in *Baseball Magazine,* Latham said that he had in fact been the benefactor of the first Louisville Slugger custom-made bat. Latham was a renowned base stealer, and his career total of 739 is still eighth-best in Major League Baseball history. But Latham was also a practical joker who enjoyed being the center of attention, so it is difficult to know how serious Latham was when he described being on a baseball trip to Louisville with the Browns.

Latham said he had broken his last bat and could not find any bats for sale in the city. Finding his way to the nearby Hillerich family woodworking shop, Latham said he asked Bud Hillerich to make him one. The woodworking apprentice was said to have obliged, making history—if you believe this version of the story. Bud Hillerich did seem to verify Latham's account in a personal letter written in 1942, four years before his death, but family members and historians note he had a sense of humor as well, and they speculate he may have just been joining in Latham's fun, stoking the story with more speculation.

Another version of the story behind the first Louisville Slugger bat suggests that Bud Hillerich's father made a bat for his amateur ballplayer son, who took the bat to games in the 1880s and showed it off to friends. One friend he played with is said to have been Gus Weyhing, a local boy himself who first broke in with Philadelphia and became a major league pitching star. As Weyhing's teammates tried the bat, they found it superior and requested Hillerich deliver more, according to this version.

Each story, true or not, has its place in history, and over the years each became part of the game's fabric, in much the same way that the legend of Ruth calling a home-run shot in the 1932 World Series lives on to this day. Whether it was Browning, Latham, or Weyhing who actually took the first swings with a Louisville Slugger bat in a professional game does not really matter; what remains is the wooden bat's place in the game's legend and lore.

EXPANDING THE BUSINESS

Bud Hillerich registered the trademark name Louisville Slugger in 1894—the bat was originally named the Falls City Slugger in reference to Louisville's location at the falls of the Ohio River. J. Frederich Hillerich was suspicious of his son's divergent path in the woodshop, forsaking the making of top-selling products such as the popular swinging butter churn and wooden bowling balls in pursuit of his passion for wooden bats. J. Frederich thought the sport of baseball was beneath the dignity of the family business and the

making of bats was a distraction, a low-margin opportunity, and certainly not something that should be the focus of a mainstream company. But Bud Hillerich loved baseball and the business of baseball. He hurt his shoulder and had to give up playing, so making bats kept him in touch with the game he cherished. Even in his disapproval, however, his father did not completely rebuke his son, allowing him to concentrate on the bat business while casting a watchful eye along the way.

"J. Fred gave Bud a hard time," says Hillerich & Brasdsby CEO John Hillerich IV, Bud Hillerich's great-grandson. "He just didn't like the business."

Bud Hillerich's love of the game proved to be a perfect match for his entrepreneurial spirit. Not content with simply making one bat after another, he sought continual improvement from the start. Hillerich invented a centering device for a lathe and an automatic sander to make crafting bats easier. Players responded, ordering Louisville Sluggers by the dozen. The bat business became so popular that J. Frederich could no longer deny either its progress or its potential and made his son Bud a partner in the business in 1897 while changing the company name to J.F. Hillerich & Son.

Butter churns, bedposts, and bowling balls would no longer be the centerpiece of the family woodworking business. The evolution of a nation and of a sport was underway, and Bud Hillerich's Louisville Slugger bats were coming along for the ride.

1875

J.F. HILLERICH MOVES HIS WOODWORKING BUSINESS TO FIRST STREET BETWEEN MAIN AND MARKET STREETS IN LOUISVILLE

1894

"LOUISVILLE SLUGGER" IS REGISTERED AS A FEDERAL TRADEMARK

1897

BUD'S CONTRIBUTION IS ACKNOWLEDGED WHEN THE COMPANY NAME IS CHANGED TO J.F. HILLERICH & SON

Since 1884, handmade bats have been crafted to precise weights, lengths, and diameters requested by players. Bat model and specifications for each player are kept on cards by Hillerich & Bradsby. More than 20,000 such cards are on file; computers now assist the lathe operator in meeting more exacting specifications.

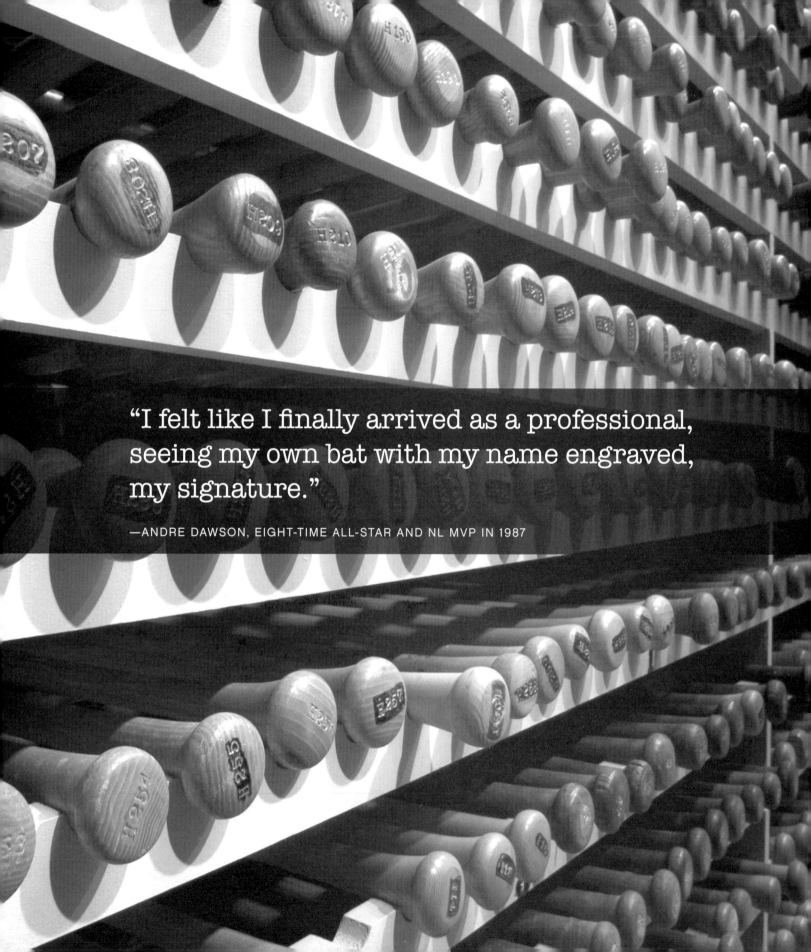

"I felt like I finally arrived as a professional, seeing my own bat with my name engraved, my signature."

—ANDRE DAWSON, EIGHT-TIME ALL-STAR AND NL MVP IN 1987

2

Evolution of the Game

By the dawn of the 20th century, baseball was no longer just a captivating game between colorful, regional rivals. Heroes were being made on playing diamonds throughout America as the game grew into a national sport at the same time the country's economic fortunes exploded.

The nation was rapidly evolving into a world economic power at the height of the Industrial Revolution. Henry Ford was building cars in Detroit. Telephones were being installed in homes and businesses by the thousands. The Wright brothers were building their first experimental airplane models, preparing to take flight. Concurrently, a 23-year-old baseball player with a keen eye, quick hands, and a prolific swing was about to take Louisville and the nation by storm. His name was Honus Wagner.

The owner of the American Association's Louisville Colonels at the time was a German Jewish immigrant named Barney Dreyfuss. Dreyfuss had moved to the United States in the late 1880s, and after becoming a successful entrepreneur, he bought part ownership in the Colonels in 1889. Dreyfuss needed a staff to manage the team and decided to hire a Louisville sportswriter he was fond of named Harry Pulliam.

A lawyer by training but working at the time as a journalist, Pulliam was hired by Dreyfuss as secretary of the Colonels. Later, Pulliam would gain his fame for his role as president of the National League from 1903 to 1909, but his first coup was undoubtedly recognizing young Honus Wagner's talent, which ultimately brought the player to Louisville for three years.

BASEBALL'S FLYING DUTCHMAN

Born in Pittsburgh in 1874 to German immigrants Peter and Katheryn Wagner, awkward but fleet-footed Johannes Peter Wagner was one of nine children. Called Hans by his mother—a moniker that later evolved into his more familiar and American Honus—Wagner was a grade-school dropout who worked in Pennsylvania's coal mines and played sandlot baseball with family and friends. His oldest brother, Albert "Butts" Wagner, was known as an outstanding baseball player with superior talents to those of his gangly brother Hans. Al Wagner played professionally briefly, and when his team needed help in 1895, he talked a team owner into giving his younger brother a tryout. Hans played for five teams his first year in the Inter-State League, then was signed in 1896 by owner Edward Barrow of the Atlantic League.

Despite his reputation as an awkward athlete, Barrow found the young player was far superior and outplayed virtually every player on every team, including his own. Wagner was eager to break into the National League, but scouting was rudimentary in these early years of professional baseball. With limited budgets, most teams had little in the way of personnel outside of a manager, so finding fresh talent was often done through word of mouth.

Such was the case for Wagner's breakthrough in the big leagues. Fellow Atlantic League competitor Claude McFarlan played for Norfolk and was impressed by Wagner in competition. McFarlan was a native Kentuckian, and because Harry Pulliam had done a favor for him years before,

McFarlan contacted Pulliam and suggested he sign a player named Honus Wagner.

Pulliam did not respond, but McFarlan would not give up. In the six games he had faced Wagner, Wagner had excelled, hitting a double, two triples, and two home runs. Convinced Wagner should be with the Colonels, he continued contacting Pulliam, sending collect telegrams and repeated letters. When Pulliam finally answered, it was only to tell McFarlan the team could not afford to accept so many collect messages. Finally, Pulliam agreed to scout Wagner.

By the time Pulliam and Colonels manager Fred Clarke saw Wagner play, word on the budding young German phenom was already out, and other teams were scouting him as well. In front of the assembled scouts, Wagner had two hits but did nothing spectacular, and Pulliam left unimpressed. In response, Pulliam sent McFarlan a collect message of his own:

"Saw your miracle play today. Don t bother me any more about him. Whatever gave you the idea that anybody with such gates-ajar legs can play baseball? I m sending you this collect, darn your hide. Let it be a lesson to you. It s lovely weather we are having, is it not?"

Curiosity got the better of Pulliam, however, and after watching Wagner play more games, he was intrigued enough to finally offer to purchase Wagner's contract from his current team. Pulliam had come to understand that Wagner's gait, which appeared awkward, was just his unique style. The player was anything but awkward.

Wagner's team at first refused Pulliam's offer, believing its star player was worth more money. But when the team fell on hard financial

Honus Wagner's career included 15 consecutive seasons batting over .300 and a lifetime average of .327. His 1909 baseball card sold for a record $2.8 million in 2007.

gentleman just six years his elder who was making custom bats for many of the players on his new team—Bud Hillerich.

Three years before and a decade after turning his first bat, Hillerich had trademarked the Louisville Slugger name and had established a tradition of engraving the trademark name on each bat, with the player's name or initials usually etched into the handle or barrel with a carving knife. Wagner liked the look and the feel of the ash bats made by Hillerich, so he, too, played with the Louisville Slugger, batting .338 his first season and just under .300 his second season. The National League contracted in 1900, shrinking from 12 teams to eight, and the Louisville Colonels was one of the disbanded franchises. As a result, Barney Dreyfuss bought controlling interest of the Pirates and took Pulliam, Wagner, and 14 other Colonels players to Pittsburgh.

For Wagner, the move was a trip home, but for Hillerich the end of the Colonels meant the end of Major League Baseball in Louisville. He would stay in close contact with both Wagner and the game, however.

A COMPETITIVE BUSINESS

At the turn of the century, America was in the midst of a population explosion. Millions of immigrants from countries including Germany, Russia, Ireland, and Italy doubled America's population from 36 million in 1870 to 80 million in 1900. The transplanted citizenry, weighted with Jewish and Irish immigrants, came ready to work, fueling the country's shift from agricultural production to

times, they began looking for someone to buy Wagner's contract. In the summer of 1897, Pulliam boarded a train and traveled to Paterson to sign Wagner, who was batting .379 with 61 runs in 74 games. For the sum of $2,100, Wagner was acquired to play for the Louisville Colonels, a fortuitous marriage in the annals of baseball history. In Louisville, Wagner became friends with a local

industrialized manufacturing, making everything from the first automobiles and telephones to new homes and roadways. No country equaled America's economic strength, as the country's standard of living had become the highest in the world.

Although the nation's new citizenry came from diverse backgrounds, millions shared a love for baseball. The sport was a unifier, bridging mixed labor pools by providing common-ground, break-time chatter, and it also made good reading material for newspapers that recognized the benefits of pregame buildup and postgame analysis.

With fan interest growing, the professional leagues increased efforts to bring consistency to the game by further standardizing rules of play. Already the pitcher's mound had been moved back from 50 feet to 60 feet and six inches, and a base on balls went from nine to eight in 1880, then to seven, six, five, and finally to four in 1889. Both changes were aimed at evening the hitter's odds and providing more offense, thereby making games more exciting. Three strikes meant you were out. The ground-rule double was implemented. A bunted ball going foul became a strike, as did a foul tip.

In 1893, the Professional National Association of Baseball Players decided that the barrels of bats could no longer be sawed off flat. Flat bats used mostly for bunting gave way to a uniform round bat, and restrictions in barrel size and length made the tools easier to handle. In the late 1890s, the diameter of the bat was expanded to two and three-quarters inches; the rule in 1859 had set a maximum of two and one-half inches. Bat makers continued to experiment within the new

rules governing length and diameter, testing innovations including variations in handle thickness, putting a knob at the end of the handle, removing the knob, and even adding double knobs.

Wagon tongue wood, originally sought by players seeking a bat that could stand up to the most powerful knocks, had already yielded to other woods lighter and more suited to giving players better bat control. Hickory was sometimes used for its hardness, but bat makers eventually yielded primarily to the northern white ash that Bud Hillerich preferred and that has dominated the bat industry for more than a century. Bat speed at the time was not an issue; bat control was paramount, because offensive strategy centered on advancing runners through base hits. The out-of-the-park home run was still an uncommon way to score a run.

Bud Hillerich, though, was not satisfied merely turning wood on a lathe to make bats. He kept busy experimenting with the bat's limitations. As he refined his work, he talked to professional players firsthand at the ballpark about the finer points of hitting and began to apply for and receive a series of patents designed to make his company's bats more effective. In December 1902, Hillerich received U.S. patent number 716541 for a process that hardened the surface of the bat. His goal was to increase the distance a bat could send a ball, prevent the bat from chipping and splintering, and to improve the overall finish and appearance of the bat. Nearly two years later, in October 1904, Hillerich received patent number 771247 to modify the surface of the bat with regular indentions.

Dozens of manufacturers at the time were looking for any possible way to separate their

At the age of 24, Ty Cobb became the youngest player in American League history to reach 1,000 career hits.

product from their competitors. They included Boston's Wright & Ditson, which sold a unique double ring–handled bat; A.G. Spalding and Brothers, which marketed the popular Mushroom bat, featuring a round knob and promising even weight distribution; A.J. Reach, a sporting goods line made by a former big-league player which sold thousands of baseballs and bats; Pontiac Turning Company of Pontiac, Michigan, featuring its trademark logo of an American Indian in full headdress; and Zimmerman's Lifter, another Michigan company that later sold its bat manufacturing plant to Hillerich.

With the American economy booming and professional and amateur players alike searching for any edge that could propel them into baseball stardom, the right bat became a sought-after magic wand, something that could make or break hitters at the plate. Seeking differentiation in the crowded marketplace, bat manufacturers began to advertise customization and personalization of their products.

Among the first to do so was Wright & Ditson, which boasted of a bat "made under the personal supervision of Napoleon Lajoie" in an advertisement. A star second baseman for Cleveland,

Nap Lajoie

Standing 6'1" and weighing 195 pounds, Napoleon "Nap" Lajoie was big for a second baseman during his era. In a career that spanned from 1896 to 1916, he was known for displaying a quiet, shy personality with the exception of a few notable outbursts. Typically, when Lajoie (pronounced LAJ-a-way) had something to say, he said it on the field with his Louisville Slugger.

Born in Rhode Island of French-Canadian descent, Lajoie dropped out of school at the age of 10 and began working first in a textile mill and later as driver of a horse-drawn taxi cab, playing semiprofessional baseball during his free time. He was noticed in 1896 by a minor league professional team which signed him to a playing contract, and almost immediately he moved up to the big leagues, playing for the National League's Philadelphia Phillies.

The chiseled, hard-hitting Lajoie was a fan favorite from the start, and when the American League wanted to prove it belonged alongside the National League by signing top talent in 1901, the Philadelphia Athletics, owned by Connie Mack, lured Lajoie and several teammates to play for them. More popular among many fans at the time than legendary hitter Ty Cobb, Lajoie's reserved demeanor is ironic considering he is at the center of two historic baseball controversies.

The Phillies did not like losing star players, and the team filed a lawsuit to prevent Lajoie and others from playing in the American League. The controversy apparently did not bother Lajoie, who had his best season ever in 1901, hitting .426, which still stands as an American League record.

But on Opening Day in 1902, the Pennsylvania Supreme Court ruled that Lajoie was bound to the Phillies. The only problem, however, was that the resulting injunction was valid only in the state of Pennsylvania, where the Supreme Court held jurisdiction. To get Lajoie on the field and keep him in the American League, he was traded to Cleveland in a scheme masterminded by league president Ban Johnson. When Cleveland traveled to play Philadelphia, authorities searched the train for Lajoie but he was never there, sitting out the road trip in honor of the injunction.

By 1903, the National League and American League dropped the dispute, peacefully coexisting until joining together to form Major League Baseball. Also that year, the Cleveland team was renamed the Naps in Lajoie's honor. He performed remarkably for the franchise, becoming one of the game's most feared and respected hitters while swinging a Louisville Slugger bat adorned with his signature.

Nap Lajoie won the American League Triple Crown in 1901.

After first endorsing a bat made by Wright & Ditson, Lajoie signed with Louisville Slugger on September 12, 1905. His bat was unique, featuring two knobs at the end that helped him smoothly swing with a split-hands grip. He could place the ball almost at will, dropping hits to all fields with undeniable proficiency.

Lajoie was involved in a second controversy in 1910. After winning four batting titles, he was dueling with Cobb for a fifth when an automotive company promised a car to the batting leader and Most Valuable Player. The players were locked in a tight battle until the last day of the season when Lajoie went 8-for-8 in a season-ending doubleheader against St. Louis. The controversy erupted because the St. Louis players were giving Lajoie the hits, playing deep in the field while he bunted time and time again. Cobb had opted to sit out the final two games of the season, trying to hold onto his batting average lead, angering fans and players. The St. Louis team's response was to allow the 35-year-old Lajoie to get the hits he needed to claim the title. Lajoie took the crown, outhitting the 23-year-old Cobb by a single point (.384 to .383).

After the season, the automotive company gave each player a car, claiming both were champions. The ultimate winner, of course, was Louisville Slugger, which had both players under contract.

Lajoie was considered by many to be the playing equal of Wagner and Ty Cobb. Saying he contributed to the bat's design—which included a second knob or "shoulder" three inches from the end of the bat to provide, as the ad said, "a better grip, thus more confidence which means a better and higher salary"—provided Wright & Ditson a unique marketing tool. The distinction would not last, though.

Seeking an edge that would win the players' favor, Bud Hillerich came up with a marketing angle of his own. When his old friend Honus Wagner had moved to Pittsburgh, the shortstop's career had taken off. Wagner won his first batting championship in 1900, hitting .381. For the next several seasons, he never hit below .330, leading the team to baseball's first World Series in 1903, an event Pirates owner Barney Dreyfuss was largely responsible for creating. By 1905, Wagner was among the first of America's true sporting superstars, and Hillerich was smart enough to capitalize. On September 1, 1905, Hillerich arranged for the star player to sign an endorsement contract for Louisville Slugger.

Lajoie might have supervised the making of a bat, but Louisville Slugger was the one and only bat for Wagner, customized for the player from his first cuts at the plate years before in Louisville. So Hillerich offered Wagner an endorsement contract, and Wagner's signature was engraved on the bat, which was then sold in retail stores. Hillerich's foresight in personalizing the bat by branding the player's signature on it gave Louisville Slugger bats an advantage.

In 1905, Wagner agreed to endorse Louisville Slugger and have his signature added to the bat, starting a trend that continues more than a century later.

The second player Hillerich signed to an endorsement contract was Ty Cobb, the Georgia native who joined the Detroit Tigers in 1905. Over his 24-year career, Cobb set 90 major league records, including some that still stand a century later. A lightning rod of a baseball player both adored and abhorred by fellow players and fans alike for his hitting prowess and vicious game-day habits, Cobb was among the first players to swing multiple bats while waiting on deck so that when he held just one at the plate, it felt considerably lighter. The man who still holds the highest lifetime batting average in Major League Baseball history was naturally a welcomed addition as a Louisville Slugger endorser in October 1908.

The third player Hillerich signed to represent Louisville Slugger was Harry Davis, the American League home-run leader from 1904 to 1907 while with the Philadelphia A's. Lajoie,

1905

HONUS WAGNER SIGNS WITH LOUISVILLE SLUGGER TO CREATE THE FIRST PROFESSIONAL SPORTS ENDORSEMENT OF A CONSUMER PRODUCT, ALLOWING HIS NAME TO BE BURNED ONTO THE BAT BARREL

1908

ARGUABLY BASEBALL'S GREATEST PLAYER, TY COBB, AGREES TO SELL LOUISVILLE SLUGGER AUTOGRAPHED BATS EMBLAZONED WITH HIS NAME

25

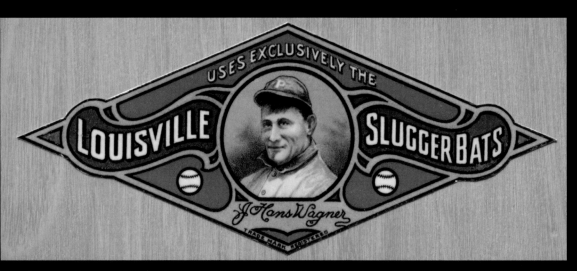

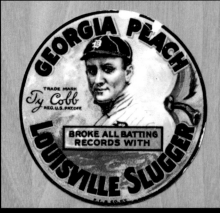

From 1916 to 1920, decals were used on Louisville Slugger bats to feature its signature players.

During one stretch of his career, Ty Cobb won the American League batting title an amazing 11 of 13 years with a Louisville Slugger in his hand.

the onetime pitchman for competitor Wright & Ditson, was the fourth. Since then, more than 8,500 professional players have signed contracts with Louisville Slugger, including greats like Babe Ruth, Ted Williams, Ernie Banks, George Brett, and Derek Jeter.

TRIAL BY FIRE

By 1910, Louisville Slugger was the preferred bat of the game's best, and J.F. Hillerich & Son were making thousands of bats sold in retail sporting goods stores throughout much of America. For 15 years, the company produced bats under a private label for one of the first giant hardware and mercantile outlets, Simmons Hardware Company of St. Louis. Representing nearly three-quarters of all company sales, these private-label bats fulfilled the amateur and youth players' need for an affordable bat.

The company's professional player bat business was managed closely by Bud Hillerich, who thrived on relationships with America's top pro players, traveling to ballparks and fraternizing with them in an effort to cultivate and maintain personal relationships and thereby keep Louisville Slugger bats in their hands. By keeping bats in the hands of the game's best players and keeping them

under endorsement contracts, Louisville Slugger–branded bats were the company's most expensive, top-quality product.

The private-label business was managed primarily by Bud Hillerich and J. Frederick Hillerich, and arranging deals with companies including Rawlings, Chicago Sporting Goods, Goldsmiths, Seattle Hardware, and the mail-order house Montgomery Ward expanded the company's business rapidly. The Buster Brown bat produced by J.F. Hillerich & Son was a top seller through a Chicago department store named Hibbard, Spencer, Bartlett & Co., known later for developing the True Value brand. But the company's biggest retail partner was Simmons Hardware. In an exclusive deal arranged between J. Frederick Hillerich and a young Simmons Hardware salesman, Frank Bradsby, J.F. Hillerich & Son gained national distribution in the largest hardware store in the world. J. Frederick Hillerich was particularly fond of Bradsby, often discussing business with him, and the relationship would prove to be long term.

A dozen or more baseball bat manufacturers existed in America, and the 25-year-old J.F. Hillerich & Son was not the biggest even with its growing

Harry "the Hat" Walker, a hitting star with the St. Louis Cardinals in the 1940s and 1950s, once toured the Hillerich & Bradsby plant. Noticing a bat in a tank of dark stain, Walker pulled it out, shook the bat, and said he liked it. From then on, bats for Walker carried a partial two-tone stain. Today, this look is referred to as "the Walker Finish," one of seven different finishes a player can order for his or her bat.

private-label business. Still, Louisville Slugger was earning a reputation as the best. Blending its stronghold on professional players with large-scale, lower-end retail bat-making, the company had earned a national presence in America's new pastime.

Despite the growth of its business, Louisville Slugger maintained a personal relationship with players at any level. For example, young men would commonly walk into the factory from off the street, holding their own planks of cured wood, asking J.F. Hillerich & Son to make a bat to their specifications. Typically, the young man entered the factory, giving instructions throughout the customization process amid flying sawdust and loud noise before leaving with his dream-making bat in hand. He would play with this bat until it wasted into splinters, patching cracks along the way with nails and tape to keep it intact as long as possible.

Like the game of baseball, however, business is a game of difficult odds. Most entrepreneurial companies never last a decade, much less a quarter of a century. Those that do understand good times rarely last without interruption. Such was the case for J.F. Hillerich & Son when good fortune turned to near-cataclysmic disaster in 1910.

As a wood-turning factory, the red brick building that housed J.F. Hillerich & Son in downtown Louisville was especially susceptible to fire. Dried wood was stacked throughout the structure, and wood shavings littered planks of flooring beneath exposed beams. Treated wood in the factory yard was stacked in rows 40 feet high, and piles of wood and wood scraps, moved through the building on steel-wheeled hand-trolleys, were scattered throughout a building constructed in 1864.

Eddie Collins was one of the first players contracted to endorse Louisville Slugger.
Photo courtesy of AP Images

Eddie Collins

Nicknamed "Cocky" for his confident on-field demeanor, Eddie Collins compiled 3,315 hits during a Major League Baseball career that spanned from 1906 to 1930, but Louisville Slugger employees remember him most for the finicky demands he made when it came to his bats.

Among Louisville Slugger's original endorsers, Collins led the Philadelphia Athletics to three World Series championships between 1910 and 1914 before being sold to the Chicago White Sox, where he finished his playing career as one of the game's all-time greats. Like most prolific hitters, Collins had specific input regarding his bats, wanting each to be made from the perfect piece of wood. He was said to be "fussy" about his bats and wanted every single one made with wood from the heart of the tree.

J.F. Hillerich & Son obliged, of course, even though the wood selection made his bats red on one side and white on the other. Such direct input from players was commonplace in the early days, and the company that has long prided itself in serving the player simply met demands then as it still does today, accommodating a myriad of special requests as long as they fit within the rules of the game.

For Collins, this meant searching through mounds of wood for just the right cut. With his crafted Louisville Slugger in hand, Collins became one of baseball's all-time great leadoff hitters, blending adept hitting with speed and base running. He was inducted into the National Baseball Hall of Fame in 1939.

1910

A DISASTER STRIKES AS FIRE SEVERELY DAMAGES THE MANUFACTURING FACILITIES OF J.F. HILLERICH & SON

The J.F. Hillerich & Son factory on Clay Street. In 1910, a fire swept through the factory on Preston Street.

Nobody knows how the fire started on Preston Street in December 1910, but a fireman on watch at the nearby No. 9 Engine Company spotted the blaze in progress. According to a newspaper article, the fire burned the factory "like paper" and raged for eight hours before firemen could bring the flames under control in freezing weather. The factory was full of bats for its upcoming spring shipment, and the inventory loss was heavy. When the smoke finally drifted away before sunset, a badly damaged factory was revealed and a company loss exceeding $50,000 was calculated.

The second floor was totally destroyed, yet much of the first floor, including equipment, tools, and wood billets used for making bats, was saved.

Perhaps most importantly, all of the model bats used to craft the personalized bats for the company's most prized customers, including Honus Wagner and Ty Cobb, were saved. When the embers finally cooled on December 13, J. Frederick and Bud Hillerich were considering the future of the family business. They were not sure whether to rebuild, relocate, or close down. In the end, they believed a new direction was in store for

After retiring from baseball in 1917, Wagner served as hitting coach for the Pittsburgh Pirates from 1933 to 1952.

"I have not considered the question of rebuilding and cannot say at present what our plans will be. We employed between 40 and 50 men, and some of them will be thrown out of work temporarily."

—BUD HILLERICH, AFTER FIRE BURNED DOWN HIS COMPANY'S LOUISVILLE MANUFACTURING FACILITY IN 1910

3

Hillerich Teams with Bradsby

J. Frederich and Bud Hillerich had begun their careers as skilled woodworkers, making refined bedposts and persnickety butter churns with smooth rounds and precise lines. As they became artisans in the craft of bat-making, the father and his son taught the several dozen men and teenagers who manned the company's Louisville factory that details were what mattered most.

For example, when Ty Cobb placed an order for his Louisville Slugger model 40TC—the TC stands for Cobb's initials, as all first-edition models are named after the player who orders them—the Hillerichs demanded their workers meet Cobb's dimensions precisely. The length was to be exactly 34½ inches long, the weight 32 ounces, the grain perfectly treated to create a two-tone appearance, and the Louisville Slugger stamp and accompanying Ty Cobb image carefully placed.

Making a wooden bat by hand worthy of serving an all-time great like Ty Cobb and to exacting dimensions was not an easy task, however. The dimly lit, sawdust-filled J.F. Hillerich & Son factory was a typical turn-of-the-century metropolitan labor shop. Punctuated by the continual buzzing of saws, craftsmanship and careful attention was a demand of the tallest order in the hand-turning room.

Steam-powered lathes whirred while diligent workers stood hand-spinning timber billets, wood shavings flying through the air. Workers typically had to check and recheck against the nearby model bat from which the order was placed, smoothing and re-smoothing the crafted bat a dozen or more times to make sure specifications matched exactly. Typically, Louisville Slugger bats in this era were heavy, becoming of the dead-ball era of baseball when the base runner predated the slugger. When finished, each bat was always stamped with the full company brand inside the oval: "Louisville Slugger, Made by J.F. Hillerich & Son, Louisville, KY."

Bats were handcrafted from billets approximately 37 inches long and about three inches in diameter.

Overseeing production, J. Frederich Hillerich and Bud Hillerich wanted bats produced in their factory to be identical to the bats they made beginning in 1884, with a watchful eye and a patient hand. During a meticulous, 30-minute process, a skilled worker could transform a billet into a game-ready weapon with a well-defined sweet spot.

After the company's factory burned to the ground, however, the Hillerichs faced a professional and personal crossroads. Money for reinvestment was tight, especially in the interest of protecting J. Frederich's retirement. To date, the family partnership had worked well enough, even if the father never completely trusted the business instincts of his baseball-impassioned son. J. Frederich understood the art of woodworking, and Bud had a way of connecting that to the intricacies of the player. He took orders directly from the players, writing the bat specifics on cards he kept in files and which the company maintains more than a century later. But Bud Hillerich never completely won his father's confidence, and his father never wanted to turn the entire business over to him. Bud was good at carousing and socializing with players and taking their bat orders, but his father believed running the business was a different proposition.

After the fire, J.F. Hillerich & Son began to rebuild, continuing to make bats while warding off competitors who poached the company's leading endorsement names with knockoff models. To combat them, a newspaper advertisement ran in the spring of 1911 after the winter fire, featuring Ty Cobb placing an order for a dozen new bats. It was accompanied by a stern, "notice to the trade"

**Bud Hillerich never quit tinkering with the bat-making process and never lost his
touch for crafting a bat or improving the lathes.**

Henry Bickel and Bud Hillerich worked side by side hand-turning wooden bats for decades.

The Bickel Family

Continuity is often cited as one of the secrets to Louisville Slugger's success, considering the specialized art of bat-making has been handed down from one generation to the next.

Consider, for example, the Bickel family's long connection to Hillerich & Bradsby. Henry "Papa" Bickel started working for the Hillerich family in 1881, years before the first bat was ever turned. He held the same passion for baseball that Bud Hillerich did, taking immediately to the finer aspects of craftsmanship when the Hillerichs began making bats in search of the perfect game-day weapon. Bickel often worked with a heavy lathe made with a wooden bed and supported by wooden legs. He worked for the company for 57 years and introduced his son, 14-year-old Fritz, to the manufacturing floor in 1912. Fritz Bickel earned $3.75 a week, a sum he considered substantial reward for hand-turning bats for baseball greats such as Ty Cobb, Honus Wagner, and Lou Gehrig.

Fritz, who worked at Hillerich & Bradsby for 50 years, once stayed up most of the night making bats for Babe Ruth who, according to legend, was scheduled to make a visit to the plant the next day. Proud of his work, Fritz laid out the bats for Ruth to see. The slugger picked them up one by one, dropping them on the floor to hear the reverberating rings.

"They aren't worth a damn," Ruth reportedly said, walking away.

Ruth was pulling Fritz's leg, of course. He loved the bats and used the handmade bats throughout 1927, the year he hit 60 home runs.

Eventually Fritz's nephew, Augie Bickel, was hired by Hillerich & Bradsby and worked there from 1931 to 1973. Augie was passionate about bat-making and Louisville Slugger in particular, taking great pride in the tools of the trade and nostalgia surrounding both. He could talk about Louisville Slugger and bat-making as long as anybody would listen, passing along that passion to workers like Danny Luckett, known and still working today as Hillerich & Bradsby's most experienced wooden bat artisan.

Combined, Henry Bickel, Fritz Bickel, and Augie Bickel worked at Hillerich & Bradsby for 149 years, making hundreds of thousands of wooden bats by hand. Their legacy continues today with Luckett and company employees applying their craftsmanship, passion, and attention to detail.

Henry Bickel was the first of three generations of Bickels to make bats for Hillerich & Bradsby.

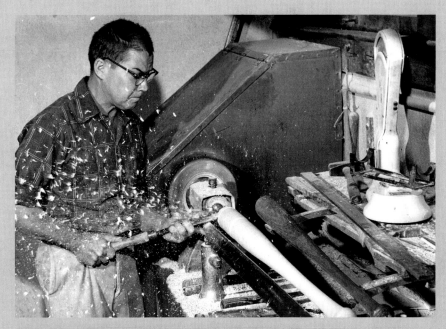

Augie, Henry Bickel's grandson, worked on Louisville Slugger bats for 42 years.

37

warning that stated the company was "running with a larger capacity than ever" with a stock of "seasoned material larger than all other factories combined."

Despite the advertisement, the company was wounded by the fire, as insurance covered only part of the Hillerich family's financial losses, and the loss of seasonal business strictly limited its cash flow. The company's business had grown in the early 20th century, but profits had been meager considering the bat company's national exposure. A primary reason, perhaps, is that the company's private-label bat business accounted for 74 percent of its sales, reducing profits.

While other companies merely slapped their logo on ordinary bats and marked them up at retail, the Hillerichs' private-label products were high quality. Bats were still a commodity at the time, because Bud Hillerich's marketing strategy of gaining top professional player endorsements was still in its infacy. Brand names like Louisville Slugger were not well known yet outside of professional baseball, and even when J.F. Hillerich & Son attempted to gain more shelf space for its brand-name bats in retail stores, these bats competed directly against the company's own private-label bats.

Take the Buster Brown bat, for example. J.F. Hillerich & Son sold these private-label bats to Hibbard, Spencer, Bartlett & Co. for 30¢ a dozen. The retailer marked them up sometimes to as much as 10¢ each—a 400 percent increase. The products were top-notch, but someone else was making most of the money. On the other hand, the Louisville Slugger Junior, a brand-name bat,

sold for $2 a dozen, delivering J.F. Hillerich & Son a profit of 80¢ a dozen. The challenge was finding a way to give customers a reason to buy the company's brand-name bats.

J. Frederich Hillerich consulted with Frank Bradsby, the Simmons Hardware salesman who helped the company grow during the years before the fire, about increasing the company's retail presence nationally. Bradsby understood the value of the Hillerich's bat-making abilities and the established Louisville Slugger brand, so when Hillerich talked to him about buying the company, Bradsby seized the opportunity.

A NEW DIRECTION

Born in Lebanon, Illinois, in 1878, Frank Bradsby moved with his family to St. Louis seven years later. He attended high school until the age of 15, quitting because he was eager to get a job. He found work at Simmons Hardware, known nationally for its quality tools and home and outdoor products, leaving at the age of 20 to fight in the Spanish-American War for the United States Army. When Bradsby returned to work for Simmons after his stint in the service, he became a prolific company salesman, eventually taking over responsibility for all sporting goods equipment for the retailer.

Bradsby was an outdoorsman who loved deep-sea fishing and horse racing but maintained grooming, polish, and poise that would have served him well had he worked on Wall Street. Instead, he excelled on Main Street, understanding the connections between sales, service, product from the manufacturer, and the individual retail

"[Bud Hillerich] was sold out of the business."
—Jack Hillerich, Bud's grandson and Chairman of the Board at Hillerich & Bradsby Co.

Frank Bradsby used his genius for sales and marketing to help make Louisville Slugger the nation's top bat maker.

customer. Bradsby also recognized the nation was becoming increasingly passionate about its leisure time and had the money to finance it. Such talk inspired J. Frederich Hillerich. In his sixties and unwilling to hand the company over to his son, Hillerich effectively sold Bud Hillerich out of ownership in 1911. For the sum of $125,000, J.F. Hillerich sold controlling interest in all facets of the business, including machinery, brand, and receivables, to 33-year-old Frank Bradsby, who moved from St. Louis to Louisville to run the bat maker. The company was renamed J.F. Hillerich & Sons Company.

Fortunately for the company and the Hillerich family, Bradsby had as much business acumen as he did sales savvy. He knew Bud Hillerich was

the backbone of the bat business, so he hired him immediately as company president and sold him back part of the business that once belonged solely to his family. Bradsby handled the sales, marketing, and overall strategy for the business, while Bud Hillerich focused on what he did best—maintaining relationships with the key professional players while making sure their bats were built to their individualized demands. The duo would prove a powerful force in American baseball and the sporting goods business in the 20th century, propelling Louisville Slugger from the middle of a crowded pack of bat makers to the top of the industry.

MARKETING STRATEGY MAKES A DIFFERENCE

Frank Bradsby was a pioneer in product promotion, far ahead of the production-era mentality that lasted in America until the 1930s, a philosophy that relied directly on the customer to dictate desired products and product attributes. Working for an innovative market leader like Simmons Hardware, he learned the benefits of product leverage. Retailers wanted his new company's private-label bats, but Bradsby made a decision to push more of the company's branded Louisville Slugger bats to those accounts in return for the business.

Ending the exclusive relationship with his old employer Simmons Hardware, Bradsby required that every retailer buying three of the company's private-label bats also purchase one of the higher-quality Louisville Slugger bats. Within just a few years, sales of the more profitable Louisville Slugger bats increased from 6.5 percent of total sales in

1911

FRANK BRADSBY, A SALESMAN FOR THE SIMMONS HARDWARE COMPANY, JOINS THE COMPANY TO HELP IT FIGHT BACK FROM LOSSES RESULTING FROM THE FIRE

1907 to more than 33 percent in 1912. Bradsby's push was not the only reason Louisville Slugger bats did well, of course. Baseball was soaring in popularity in America, and the company's star endorsement strategy was taking hold. So were sporting goods sales in general, however, and with the marketplace growth came a doubling of bat manufacturers in the United States.

The new competitors seemed to spring up everywhere, from the Northeast to the Deep South. In Athens, Georgia, the Hanna Manufacturing Company, a wood-turning specialist that primarily made handles for tools such as shovels and farm implements, jumped into the bat business. The company experimented with the available and abundant hickory and southern ash, but eventually arrived at the same conclusion that other manufacturers had already reached—northern white ash makes the best bats. Like Hillerich, Hanna purchased lands in New York and Pennsylvania to supply wood for bat-making (the company manufactured bats under the Batrite and Hanna brands until the early 1970s, when the advent of aluminum bats dried up primary markets).

When Louisville Slugger sales began to flatten in 1913 from the increased competition, Bradsby went back to planning. Baseball was no longer a game played by blue-collar men. The game's rising popularity combined with the nation's increasing wealth meant more children had time and money for playing games and buying sporting goods. Teenage boys did not have to work; they now attended school. And after school and on weekends, they had time to emulate their sporting heroes, most always baseball players.

Some of the earliest companies entering the youth market, like A.J. Reach and Company, sold cheap, machine-made bats made from left-over goods, believing price mattered more than quality. These products had little or nothing in common with those used in the professional leagues. On the contrary, quality and a connection to the big-league game was Louisville Slugger's strength from the day the Hillerichs turned their first bat. Thus, Bradsby sought to leverage the company's strength in professional bats in the youth market.

The autographed bats popular with adults were sold to youth, only as junior models. Previously, the company had offered the Louisville Slugger Junior, but its price point was high and without a star player's signature, the value seemed low. But after putting autographed Louisville Slugger Juniors on sale in 1914, the bats were in high national demand within two years. Youngsters wanted to emulate Ty Cobb and other great players of the game. Arriving at the sandlot or the ballfield with an authentic bat, one endorsed by the great himself, lent cache. And the more youth autographed bats the company sold, the more adult autographed bats the company sold. By 1916, sales of the brand-name Louisville Slugger bats had increased by more than 600 percent.

That same year, Bradsby renamed the company Hillerich & Bradsby in honor of its success. Immediately upon changing the company's name, the logo placed on its branded bats changed in accordance: "Louisville Slugger, Hillerich & Bradsby, Louisville, KY." Bradsby made another drastic change to the company that year, adding

1916

Frank Bradsby (right) hosted American League president William Harridge at the Hillerich & Bradsby factory during the 1934 winter baseball meetings.

golf equipment to its lineup. Bradsby and Bud both loved the game, and Bradsby was confident it would become the next big thing in America. Manufacturing golf clubs at Hillerich & Bradsby's Louisville factory, the company made an immediate impact in the industry, expanding its scope beyond baseball bats and diversifying its business.

In hindsight, the timing for the company's entry into the youth market could not have been better. Baseball was hitting its stride as a national sport. For years, the game had plodded along during the dead-ball era, in which consistent hitters and scrappy base runners were often the stars on offense while pitchers usually stole the show in the

When Babe Ruth reached for a bat, he always grabbed a Louisville Slugger.

Ruth thrilled Yankees fans from 1920 to 1934.

"I never heard a crowd boo a homer, but I've heard plenty of boos after a strikeout." —BABE RUTH

field. Among the game's more promising young pitchers in 1916 was a young Boston Red Sox left-hander named George Herman Ruth Jr.

THE BIRTH OF AN AMERICAN SPORTS LEGEND

As part owner of the bat manufacturer and then as the company's president, Bud Hillerich could no longer be the sole face of the company in the eyes of every professional player. So many teams playing in so many cities meant somebody else had to become the primary representative of Louisville Slugger to the professional game. A neophyte in the company factory sweeping floors in 1901, Henry Morrow became for Louisville Slugger what Bud Hillerich was before it— the players' bridge to the company. He attended spring training every season, greeting the players at the ballfields and hanging out with them in restaurants and clubs after games. During the season, he returned to Louisville, traveling from there to another 50 games, seeking to spend time with current players under contract as well as those whom the company was interested in signing to endorsement deals.

The players respected Morrow, who represented Louisville Slugger in professional baseball for 30 years. Among Morrow's more memorable professional achievements was inking Babe Ruth to a Louisville Slugger endorsement contract in 1918 for the sum of $100. Although the move looks like the bargain of the century almost 100 years later, Ruth was not yet known as a great hitter when Morrow signed him.

Playing for the Boston Red Sox, Ruth was primarily a pitcher in the early part of his career. In 1916, Ruth won 23 games against 12 losses, with an earned-run average of 1.75. Ruth's numbers on the mound were similar in 1917 (24–13, 2.01 ERA). But in 1918, Ruth's pitching appearances declined and Boston used him mostly as an outfielder. Perhaps that is because during the previous two years, Ruth's limited appearances as a batter began to reveal a prowess at the plate that surpassed his pitching ability. With a Louisville Slugger in hand, Ruth appeared at the plate more than 300 times, batted .300, and led the American League in home runs (11).

Ruth topped that performance in 1919. He was the first player to order a bat from Louisville Slugger with a knob at the end of the handle; thus, he is generally credited with contributing to the development of the modern baseball bat. Hillerich & Bradsby gladly made the bat for Ruth, continuing its custom-made tradition. With the R43 model, Ruth slugged his way to a single-season home-run record with 29. At the time, many baseball observers considered the rare feat untouchable. Ruth, however, had another idea. He realized fans loved the out-of-the-park bash and planned to keep swinging for the fences.

Having the best and most promising professional players representing Louisville Slugger was not enough to completely set Hillerich & Bradsby apart from its competitors, however. Previously, Hillerich & Bradsby relied on relationships between its sales force and the retailer to place product on shelves, but Bradsby determined demand needed to be created at the

1917

HONUS WAGNER, THE FIRST PLAYER TO ENDORSE AN AUTOGRAPHED SLUGGER BAT, SETS A RECORD WITH 3,430 CAREER HITS

1919

A NATIONAL AD
CAMPAIGN BEGINS A
FOUR-YEAR RUN THAT
HELPS HILLERICH
& BRADSBY GROW
DRAMATICALLY

1923

HILLERICH & BRADSBY
BECOMES THE TOP
BAT MAKER IN THE
NATION, SELLING
140,000 DOZEN BATS;
TY COBB BREAKS
WAGNER'S RECORD
BY REACHING 3,455
HITS

Rogers Hornsby, perhaps the greatest shortstop to ever play the game, used a 36" Louisville Slugger bat.

a marketing strategy that trumpeted players as role models, the pamphlet featured statistics and facts from the 1918 season, tips on playing the game, and messages from top endorsing players such as Ty Cobb, who suggested he got more hits because he played with Louisville Slugger bats. During the four-year national campaign, Hillerich & Bradsby also introduced a slogan designed to inspire youth to emulate their heroes. "Ask the bat boy, he knows," suggested that the one handling bats for the best players knew well and sure what bats they were swinging— Louisville Slugger.

The advertising campaign proved to be exactly what Hillerich & Bradsby needed to make its baseball bat the national leader. By 1923, the company had thrown down the gauntlet and left competitors behind, soaring from total annual bat sales of roughly 23,000 dozen in 1919 to more than 140,000 dozen—an increase of more than six times over. During the same period, sales of Louisville Slugger and the company's higher-quality and more expensive autographed bats rose at the same rate as overall bat sales. With more than 1 million sold in total, Hillerich & Bradsby became the undisputed world leader in baseball bat manufacturing.

Timing is everything, of course, in both business and sport. The fortuitous rise of Ruth and baseball's slugging era at precisely the same time the company stepped onto the national advertising stage to promote its star-worthy bats could not have been better coordinated.

Then, in 1920 Babe Ruth debuted in New York City, one of the world's biggest markets, after being traded from the Red Sox for $100,000 in cash.

consumer level so that retailers would be compelled to carry Louisville Slugger bats. The company had the game's best brand; they just needed to put the brand to work. Most companies operating in the crowded sporting goods market advertised. So in an effort to better compete nationally, the company launched a national advertising and promotion campaign in 1919 aimed specifically at the youth market.

Advertising in stalwart, male-oriented national publications such as *The Sporting News, Boys Life,* and *Popular Mechanics,* ads were placed by Hillerich & Bradsby during the prime spring baseball months. At the same time, the company published an informational and inspirational pamphlet named *Famous Sluggers.* Implementing

With the Yankees, Ruth left pitching behind, emerging as one of the greatest hitters to ever play the game. In his first season in New York, Ruth hit 54 home runs, batted .376, and set a slugging percentage mark (.847) that stood as a Major League Baseball record for more than 80 years. The next season, Ruth had perhaps his best year ever at the plate, hitting 59 home runs while batting .378 and leading the Yankees into the 1921 World Series (the team lost five games to three against the New York Giants after Ruth was hurt in Game 2, which hampered his play in the rest of the series).

Ruth was big (some said overweight), and he had the strength to whip Louisville Slugger lumber through the strike zone, driving balls farther out of the park than fans were used to. They began to associate long home runs by other professional players as "Ruthian" feats. The game changed, becoming a power hitter's contest. Ruth was the star of this new show, emerging as America's first national sports hero and legend. When he stepped to the plate, America took notice. And every time he caused a collective pause by taking one of his massive swings, the bat in his hands was a Louisville Slugger.

Ruth was not, of course, the first or only big-league star taking Louisville Sluggers to the plate. Cobb, one of the company's first endorsers, had arguably passed his prime in 1923, the year Hillerich & Bradsby became the largest bat manufacturer in the world, but his career accomplishments continued to pile up. When Cobb passed Honus Wagner's career record with 3,455 hits by the end of the 1923 season, it was especially validating for Bud Hillerich, since most of Wagner's and Cobb's hits came using the company's custom-made bats.

J. Frederich Hillerich had been reluctant to enter the baseball business almost 40 years before, and he often doubted his son's instincts for serving the game. But he did live to see Louisville Slugger rise to prominence within America's pastime, with top players such as Ruth, Cobb, and Wagner making the company's bat their personal choice when standing at the plate. The following winter, in 1924, J. Frederich Hillerich slipped on an icy Louisville street and fell, then became ill during his recovery. He died soon after, but his legacy of customized craftsmanship in baseball was well established.

1924

COMPANY FOUNDER J. FREDERICH SLIPS ON AN ICY STREET AND SOON PASSES AWAY

The Cincinnati Reds once sought the expertise of Hillerich & Bradsby during a hitting slump. The Reds got a new supply of Louisville Slugger bats and some advice: let the bats lie in the sun outside the dugout. The team did, and the Reds pulled out of their hitting slump and became ardent fans of Louisville Slugger bats. The "advice" turned out to be from a Louisville Slugger employee who believed baseball to be 90 percent psychological.

After six years with Boston, Babe Ruth's contract was sold to the Yankees, where he proceeded to hit more homers than the entire Red Sox team combined for 10 of the next 12 years.

"I swing big, with everything I've got. I hit big or I miss big. I like to live as big as I can."

—BABE RUTH

4

History Making

The man known as the Sultan of Swat preferred holding a heavy piece of crafted lumber in his hands when standing in at the plate. Early in his career, Babe Ruth was known to swing a 54-ounce hickory bat. By the time he went on his home-run hitting tear with the Yankees in 1927, however, he preferred a 40-ounce Louisville Slugger, a bat he felt was light enough to generate the necessary bat speed but heavy enough to give him the desired power upon impact.

The combination worked well for Ruth, whose audacious numbers at the plate led the '27 Yankees to 110 regular-season wins and a sweep of the Pittsburgh Pirates in the World Series. Bolstered by the strong performance of Yankees first baseman and cleanup hitter Lou Gehrig, Ruth got more good pitches to hit batting in the No. 3 spot and smashed a then-record 60 home runs. An endorser of Louisville Slugger himself, Gehrig knocked 47 home runs of his own to go with a .373 batting average.

In the 1920s, the population of the United States exceeded 100 million for the first time, so there was no shortage of ticket-buying fans eager to help grow the game of baseball and in the process financially reward great players like Ruth. Low-cost travel, a critical element in the growth of sports popularity, was available to more and more people as the cost of a new Ford dropped below $300. Idle talk on the street would often center on either baseball or Harry Houdini's latest feats. Movies were the rage, and the first Oscars were awarded in 1927, with the movie *Wings* winning the first award for Best Picture.

Hillerich & Bradsby employee Henry Bickel looks over bats used by legends Lou Gehrig and Babe Ruth.

1928

TY COBB LEAVES
BASEBALL WITH
4,191 CAREER HITS, A
RECORD THAT WOULD
STAND FOR DECADES

**Lou Gehrig's 23 career grand
slams still stand as a Major
League Baseball record.**

While the automobile helped to shrink the country even more than trains had, the radio finished the job, instantly taking news coast to coast into homes and diners and businesses both rural and urban. Suddenly, the crack of the bat was a sound that was instantly recognizable to all. Both the NBC and CBS networks began broadcasting baseball games on the radio. When air travel became routine, the final connections were made for large cities everywhere to enjoy sports teams that could go anywhere to meet their rivals.

The American League race had been all but over in September 1927 as the Yankees ran away from the field, so all eyes had turned to Ruth, who hit 17 home runs in the season's final month to set the home-run record and electrify fans around the country. Baseball had never seen anything like it—and neither had Hillerich & Bradsby. The company's bats were pictured in almost every photo run in magazines and newspapers throughout the season. Rarely did Ruth pose without a bat in hand, and most people following the game knew his brand of choice.

When radios were tuned in on someone's front porch or in the local barber shop, people gathered to hear about their favorite baseball teams or just to find out if the Babe had hit another home run that day. Meanwhile, the population increased another 25 percent in the 1930s, and car sales reached almost 3 million. Times were hard during the Great Depression that had begun in 1929 and continued through most of the '30s, but the powerful events of the decade drove more fans to baseball and other sports than ever before. Horse racing was legal in 21 states, another boon to Hillerich & Bradsby's home state of Kentucky. By the end of the 1930s, 80 percent of the U.S. population owned a radio, so everyone had a favorite team. Stars of the baseball diamond became household names, and arguments over the greatest players were a universal topic of conversation.

Louisville Slugger's Henry Morrow and Bud Hillerich had gone to many of the Yankees' biggest games the year Babe Ruth hit 60 home runs, including every one of the World Series contests.

Morrow and Ruth were so close, in fact, and Ruth was so pleased with the way the company kept him outfitted with his favorite bats, that he delivered a gift the company still holds among its most prized possessions.

Since Ruth swung such a heavy bat, it lasted far longer than many lightweight bats tend to today. Ruth's bats had so much wood in them that they often lasted for months without breaking. To keep track during the historic 1927 season, Ruth made notches in the wood each time he knocked a home run. Only a few of these bats are known to be in existence, but one with 21 notches resides in the Louisville Slugger Museum at the company's headquarters in Louisville, Kentucky. To this day, fans can see the actual bat Ruth used to hit one-third of his historic home-run total that year

The R43 bat Babe Ruth used in 1927 features notches he made after each home run.

"During a game in 1927, Babe cracked one of these bats and then gave it to my father as a gift. I guess Babe really liked my dad. My dad kept it for a little while but then turned it over to H&B. My dad felt it was th right thing to do."

— BILL MORROW, SON OF LONGTIME HILLERICH & BRADSBY EMPLOYEE HENRY MORROW

1932

BASEBALL'S MOST
FAMOUS HOME RUN
IS LAUNCHED WHEN
BABE RUTH "CALLS"
HIS SHOT AGAINST
THE CUBS IN THE
WORLD SERIES

1933

POWERBILT
GOLF CLUBS ARE
LAUNCHED BY
HILLERICH & BRADSBY

because he cared so much about the company that had provided it. Sports memorabilia was not as valuable in those days as it is today, but Ruth understood the symbolism of passing along the historic bat, which he gave to Morrow, his friend and contract representative.

The era was a heyday of sorts for the company, with its bats reaching an all-time high in popularity and its golf club business soaring as well. Ruth liked to spend his winters in Florida playing golf, and so did Bud Hillerich. In 1933, Hillerich & Bradsby expanded its rapidly growing golf business, naming the company's club line PowerBilt. Bud Hillerich liked providing the clubs to baseball players like Ruth, who often played with Hillerich & Bradsby's PowerBilt clubs during their off-seasons.

Olin Dutra, a professional golfer from California who played on the PGA Tour for more than 15 years and earned 19 wins, played with Hillerich & Bradsby's clubs to win the 1932 PGA Championship and then continued using the clubs after they were given the brand name PowerBilt in 1933. Dutra claimed his career-best victory at the 1934 U.S. Open in Philadelphia, overcoming a severe attack of dysentery to shoot a final round 72 with his PowerBilt clubs, beating Gene Sarazen by a single stroke.

No matter how popular or profitable golf became for the company, however, Hillerich & Bradsby never lost its focus on baseball. Bats and the players who used them had been the company's cornerstone, so even when divergent business paths were taken, attention to detail in America's game never wavered.

RELATIONSHIPS RUN DEEP

Personal bonds between Hillerich & Bradsby and the game's best players were common and often became lasting friendships. Bud Hillerich, his wife Rose, and their children Ward, John A. Jr., and Cletus led a quintessential life in the 1930s and early 1940s. Hillerich loved the game and the company so much that he worked nonstop throughout his sixties and seventies, never contemplating retirement. Hillerich did, however, enjoy the spoils of his labor, traveling, frequenting top restaurants, and playing on golf courses in some of the world's best cities. Often, his travel companions included friends from professional baseball rosters.

One particularly memorable trip for Bud and Rose Hillerich lasted from October 1934 through January 1935 during a baseball tour of Japan. Traveling on a steamship, the Hillerichs were joined by couples including Babe Ruth and his second wife, the actress and model Claire Hodgson (and her daughter Julia); Lou Gehrig and his wife Eleanor; and star Yankees pitcher Vernon Louis "Lefty" Gomez and his new wife, actress June O'Dea. Ruth had just moved from the Yankees to the Braves and would play only one more season of baseball, retiring in 1935 with 714 career home runs, most of them hit with a Louisville Slugger. Gehrig, a New York native known throughout his playing career with the Yankees for his durability, played several more sterling seasons before being diagnosed with amyotrophic lateral sclerosis (ALS), which claimed his life in 1941 at the age of 37. Rare photos of the historic trip across the Atlantic, featuring baseball's royalty posing onboard the ship and making a stop in Venice, remain in possession of the Hillerich family and have rarely been seen in public.

Frank Bradsby did not typically dabble in such public, player-fraternizing events. He did not have any children, and his life was the sporting goods business. Bradsby was a formidable figure in the industry and was among the first elected to the industry's Hall of Fame, along with such stalwarts as Ole Evinrude (inventor of the outboard boat motor), A.G. Spalding (founder of the retail company), and John Browning (inventor of the Winchester rifle). Bradsby also served for 16 consecutive terms as president of the Athletic Goods Manufacturing Association, allowing others, notably Henry Morrow and Bud Hillerich, to serve as the face of the company among players. Bradsby was more typically the face of the company in key business relationships between retailers, bankers, and other industry types. From the moment he became a part of the company's ownership, Bradsby approached its interests with complete conviction and dedication, the way a parent grooms and guides a child.

The Great Depression was hard on the city of Louisville, though perhaps not as hard as it was on other cities throughout America—following the end of Prohibition in the United States in 1933, Kentucky's largest city relied upon the growing bourbon whiskey industry to keep money flowing. With one-third of all bourbon whiskey in America coming from the Louisville area, local distilleries provided a measure of protection during hard times. One company, Louisville's Brown-Forman, even produced bourbon whiskey for medicinal purposes during Prohibition. While sales of baseball bats and golf clubs slumped, Hillerich & Bradsby managed to survive as dreams and leisure were all that kept some families going through the difficult period. However, while city residents and the business community escaped crippling damage from the financial crisis, the 100-year flood tipped the scales for many.

Water levels in the Ohio River were already on the rise in early January 1937 from melting snowfall to the north. When rain began to fall in the middle of the month at a rate of more than an inch a day on average over the span of two weeks, the frozen ground repelled the water to the river, and the rising level invaded Louisville, a city without substantial flood walls. Before subsiding in late January, the Ohio River had risen more than 50 feet in Louisville, some 10 feet above the second-highest crest ever recorded. Several feet of water crept into Hillerich & Bradsby, completely submerging the golf club–manufacturing facility. Martial law was declared across the city as looters searched abandoned properties.

Thousands of properties flooded, and more than 70 percent of the city's residents were evacuated, with half of the municipality's 64,000 homes washed out or completely washed away. No Louisville industries were closed as a result of the flood, but Hillerich & Bradsby lost precious manufacturing time before the prime spring season. Company employee Jack McGrath rowed to the office down the flooded streets of the city to assess the damage.

"For days we were paralyzed," he said, "and even following the flood things were a sorry mess.

The All-Star Cruise of 1934

In 1934, Bud Hillerich accompanied a 14-man All-Star team, along with several players' wives, on a baseball tour of Japan. Hillerich is seen here standing on the cruise ship between Lefty Gomez (right) and Babe Ruth (center).

Despite the Great Depression putting one of every four Americans out of work, baseball was exploding in popularity during the 1930s and the world was taking notice. Hillerich & Bradsby wanted to take advantage of the sport's growing interest across Asia, particularly in Japan, where baseball had been exported from American shores soon after it became all the rage.

Teaching English and American history at Tokyo University, an American professor named Horace Williams had first introduced baseball to Japan in 1873, and in the first three decades of the 20th century, amateur and high school baseball spread throughout the country. Soon after, Major League Baseball All-Star teams began traveling to Japan for exhibition games, making extra money during the off-season.

Herb Hunter, who played briefly in the major leagues for four teams during a four-year career, was among the leaders in the effort to popularize the game in Japan, taking Herb Hunter All-Stars to tour the country beginning in 1920. Three Major League Baseball players—Moe Berg, Lefty O'Doul, and Ted Lyons—were recruited to teach baseball

at Japanese universities, and citizens seemingly could not get enough of America's pastime.

After the 1934 Major League Baseball season, 14 players—many of them taking their wives—traveled with Bud Hillerich and his wife, Rose, on a trip organized by Hunter. Bud Hillerich had traveled on an earlier around-the-world baseball promotion trip in the early 1920s and saw the value of expanding interest in baseball throughout the world and Japan in particular. The group including the Hillerichs set sail for Japan from Vancouver in October 1934 aboard the 666-foot *Empress of Japan*.

The ship was loaded with crates of freshly made Louisville Sluggers, but the bats were not the stars on board. Players making the trip with the Hillerichs included Babe Ruth, Charlie Gehringer, Jimmie Foxx, Lou Gehrig, Earl Averill, and Lefty Gomez, each of whom would later be enshrined in the National Baseball Hall of Fame. The team was billed by MLB as the "Babe Ruth and Lou Gehrig All-Stars."

Perhaps the most interesting player on the cruise ship was Moe Berg, the enigmatic third-string catcher who was making his second trip to Japan. Berg would later be known as a spy for the Office of Strategic Services, the forerunner of the CIA. At the time, no one could understand why Berg was picked for the trip at the last moment. Later, his life was immortalized in Nicholas Dawidoff's book *The Catcher Was a Spy: The Mysterious Life of Moe Berg.*

The Japanese government noticed the attention that Berg gave to his camera and at one point boarded the ship and searched for his film. They also confiscated film from Ruth and others, returning it with certain buildings inked out. After World War II ended, it became known that Berg had indeed climbed to a hospital rooftop and taken pictures of buildings that he would later provide to the OSS.

The cruise ship with the Hillerichs and others aboard stopped briefly in Honolulu for a game, then arrived in Japan on November 4. Ruth, who had played his last year with the Yankees, was offered manager duties for the all-stars. He was assigned by A's owner/manager Connie Mack, who was also on the trip and wanted to audition Ruth for possibly becoming the new A's manager.

The American all-stars played against the Dai Nippon (which in 1936 became known as the Yomiuri Giants). Ultimately, no manager offer was made to Ruth, but the team won all of its games in Japan, posting a 17–0 record.

The 17 games played were spread over a month, followed by exhibition games in Shanghai and Manila. After the official tour ended, the players dispersed and returned home by different routes and means. The Hillerichs, Ruths (including daughter Julia), as well as a few others stopped in Java and Bali, then sailed through the Suez Canal to Europe, where stops included Venice, Paris, St. Moritz, and London.

Gehrig and his wife Eleanor took a different ship home, as Ruth and Gehrig had what would become a final falling out on the trip. With Ruth no longer playing for New York, years of ill feelings between two men who had started out as friends had finally came to a head.

Two years after the 1934 exhibition series, seven teams formed the Japanese Professional Baseball League. The players' preferred bat, of course, was the Louisville Slugger.

After completing their tour of Japan, the All-Stars split up and returned to the United States by different routes. Bud Hillerich (kneeling, right) and his wife Rose, Lefty Gomez and his wife June (standing, right), Babe Ruth and his wife Claire (standing, center), and friends visited Venice on the way to other stops in Europe.

During World War II, Hillerich & Bradsby's production lines
were often filled by women manufacturing M1 carbine stocks.

For example, our front office…was full of ice, mud, and broken windows, and debris was everywhere. The cleanup job was just one of the nastiest projects that we ever had to do. The first thing done was to remove to the second floor the private liquor stock of Mr. Bradsby, and some belonging to the company, that had for years been stored in the basement vault."

The company was now faced with rebuilding in the midst of the Depression. One full month of business was lost while water was pumped out and mud was cleaned from the facilities. As a man who was investing his heart and soul into the company, the 69-year-old Bradsby suffered unduly as well. He felt a heavy burden from the flood and the difficult economy. He continued working, serving with pride and passion, but died in May 1937 from a heart attack. He was on a train when he passed, traveling back from Washington, D.C., where he had lobbied for an end to the federal excise tax on sporting goods equipment.

HILLERICH TRADITION CONTINUES

Because Frank Bradsby had no immediate heirs upon his death, his ownership shares in the company transferred into a trust held in St. Louis until the Hillerich family bought them from his surviving nieces and nephews in the late 1960s. Some of his original shares had already been watered down from the period right after the flood; Bradsby had magnanimously orchestrated a plan that allowed some workers, including manufacturing laborers, to obtain small numbers of shares in lieu of pay during the cash-strapped months.

Hillerich & Bradsby ran two shifts of employees at the time, so small numbers of shares were sprinkled to numerous employee families, including some who still attend annual company shareholder meetings to this day. A small group of employees banded together in the early 1940s and attempted to take company control from president Bud Hillerich, but the plot failed and he continued running the business.

Despite the death of Frank Bradsby, Hillerich & Bradsby flourished under Bud Hillerich's leadership. The end of the Depression, combined with increased production for service to the United States military in World War II, helped the company rebound from the difficult period in the late 1930s. During the war, Hillerich & Bradsby never stopped making bats. Servicemen played baseball during their downtime, meaning bats were a hot commodity during the war. But the company also served the military itself, making M1 carbine stocks, tank pins, billy clubs, and other war-worthy gadgets simultaneously. Before the war, Hillerich & Bradsby employed more than 350 workers. After job cuts due to diminished retail demand during the war, the company still employed more than 200.

Hillerich & Bradsby and its trademark Louisville Slugger were experiencing another renaissance. More than 90 percent of all professional players in the early 1940s used a Louisville Slugger, and the company was selling more than 2 million bats annually to professional and amateur players.

Nobody in the modern era of baseball has likely loved either the game or its most vital tool

1937

A SECOND DISASTER STRIKES HILLERICH & BRADSBY WHEN THE OHIO RIVER FLOODS DOWNTOWN LOUISVILLE AND DAMAGES ITS OFFICES AND MANUFACTURING FACILITY; BRADSBY IS WORN DOWN BY THE RECOVERY EFFORT AND DIES LATER THAT YEAR

1941

MANUFACTURING IS SWITCHED TO M1 CARBINE STOCKS AND TANK PINS TO SUPPORT THE WWII EFFORT

1946

BUD HILLERICH DIES
ON HIS WAY TO THE
ANNUAL WINTER
BASEBALL MEETINGS;
HIS SON WARD
BECOMES CEO

more than Bud Hillerich. Spanning six decades, he dedicated his professional and personal life to the sport, perfecting the bat and forging and keeping relationships with players and organizations throughout professional baseball. He talked about never retiring and did not, working without interruption into his later years. In 1946, Hillerich was traveling through Chicago on his way to Los Angeles for baseball's winter meetings when, at the age of 80, he suffered a heart attack at the Palmer House and died. The Louisville Slugger brand he created more than half a century before would continue without interruption, however, thanks to two men also well established in the world of baseball.

Ward A. Hillerich, CEO, 1946–49

A CHANGE IN LEADERSHIP

Ward A. Hillerich was a familiar presence around the game of baseball and enjoyed the glamour associated with America's pastime just as his father Bud had. Already working in the company before taking over leadership of Hillerich & Bradsby upon his father's death, he was friends with the game's greats, including Babe Ruth and Ty Cobb. He understood the value of the Louisville Slugger brand began with the best players in the world and ran through the youngest amateur players. Ward Hillerich continued the company's tradition, but his term as company president was cut short when he died in late 1949 after a lengthy battle with cancer. In early 1950, Ward Hillerich's younger brother, John A. "Junie" Hillerich Jr., became president of Hillerich & Bradsby, a position he held for 20 years.

As comfortable in the clubhouse as his father and brother, Junie Hillerich immediately immersed himself in the professional game and its best players. He was a student of baseball, passing along tips to hitters and accepting feedback from players to pass along to Hillerich & Bradsby's bat makers. Once described by *Time* magazine as a "slim, gregarious Kentuckian," Hillerich had a box at the state's premier horse track, Churchill Downs, and a winter home in Sarasota, Florida. During baseball season, Hillerich traveled from city to city, fraternizing in the clubhouse like a best friend and assistant coach. Combining the "persistence of a bleacher heckler with the sympathy of a wife," he talked to players about the science of the game, seeking to help them find solutions related to the bat or the plate like a hitting coach might.

Ward A. Hillerich and Babe Ruth at the Kentucky Derby in 1934

Stan Musial

Preacher Roe, a five-time National League All-Star pitcher and known spitballer who went 44–8 during a three-year stretch in the early 1950s for Brooklyn, said of his strategy to pitch Stan Musial, "I throw him four wide ones and try to pick him off at first." Even his spitball was no match for the man known to watch pitchers so closely he could time their pitches. After he had your timing down, he was a threat to the health of your infield.

Perhaps Roe hadn't heard Musial say, "When a pitcher's throwing a spitball, don't worry and don't complain. Just hit the dry side like I do."

Perhaps the most telling statement about Stan Musial's value to his Cardinals over his 22-year career is that the statue of him that stands in front of new Busch Stadium in St. Louis is inscribed, "Here stands baseball's perfect warrior. Here stands baseball's perfect knight."

Feared by pitchers immediately upon his entry into the National League in 1941, Musial captured a stadium full of awards and recognitions—three MVP Awards (1943, 1946, and 1948), seven batting titles, and induction into the National Baseball Hall of Fame in 1969.

For each of his 3,630 hits and 475 home runs, Musial used a Louisville Slugger, a practice he began in the minor leagues. He said, "...I signed with Louisville [Slugger] back in 1941, when I was in Triple A. And whoever signed me up, I give them a lot of credit, because in those days I was still in the minor leagues...

"I always used a Louisville Slugger...but I used the thinnest bat in the majors. Louisville would send me this thin handle, then I would scrape it down and make it even thinner."

His bat handle may have been thin, but his résumé was anything but. Musial used his bat to help his team win three World Series titles, finishing in the top five in batting average every year during the 1940s save one. Then he got even better, winning the Silver Bat Award as the National League batting champion in 1950, 1951, 1952, and again in 1957, despite competing with the likes of Willie Mays, Hank Aaron, and Richie Ashburn. In 1999, the left-handed-hitting outfielder was named as one of only 30 players on the All-Century Team.

"He was a good hitter. I think the best. He had the sharpest eyes I've ever seen in a baseball hitter. Some of the boys would throw bullets up there and would throw them six inches from his nose. He wouldn't move. He wouldn't even flinch." —PREACHER ROE ON STAN MUSIAL

Cardinals outfielder Stan Musial used a Louisville Slugger bat throughout a Hall of Fame career that included three MVP Awards.

John A. "Junie" Hillerich Jr., CEO, 1950–1969

1949

WARD HILLERICH DIES
AND HIS BROTHER
JOHN A. HILLERICH
JR. TAKES OVER;
HILLERICH & BRADSBY
ESTABLISHES THE
SILVER SLUGGER
AWARD FOR THE
BATTING CHAMPIONS
OF BOTH THE
AMERICAN AND
NATIONAL LEAGUES

Understanding the sensitivity of big-league players, Hillerich delivered his sage advice with a salesman's smile and a smooth voice. When future Hall of Famer Stan Musial was playing for the St. Louis Cardinals, the 20-time All-Star selection once fell into a rare slump at the plate. Granted, a slump for Musial, who had 3,630 career hits and a lifetime batting average of .331, was not the same as it was for other players, but he was uncomfortable when standing in against a pitcher nonetheless. Hillerich made a trip to St. Louis and watched Musial at the plate. After the game, Hillerich discovered that Musial, who had complained his bats had lost their "feel," had worn down the handles on his bats a quarter of

an inch by scraping them against the dugout steps while awaiting his turn at the plate.

Junie Hillerich's son, Jack Hillerich, says his father never talked much about the ballplayers he frequently socialized with. The game had an unspoken code that even the media covering teams in those days followed. What happened on the field was fair game, but what happened off the field was off the record.

"My uncle [Ward] and Ruth apparently liked the ladies," says Jack Hillerich, smiling. "My father did tell me that. But most of what he shared was just anecdotal. Little stories here and there about what it was like then."

Young Jack Hillerich did share some experiences with several of the game's greatest players firsthand, however. His father took the family to Sarasota during professional baseball's spring training. In addition to its climate and access to the beaches, Junie chose Sarasota as a second home because the Louisville Colonels, Boston's farm team, spent spring training there. Every year on the first of January, the family loaded into two cars, making a three-day trip from Louisville to Sarasota, stopping along the way in Chattanooga, Tennessee, and South Georgia. In Sarasota, the Hillerichs' across-the-street neighbor was a baseball player named Ted Williams.

SPLENDID ADVICE

As a player obsessed with hitting, Ted Williams didn't just want a good bat or even a great bat. He wanted the very best bat, from the best wood, with the perfect weight and length. He wanted to understand what made a bat as good as it

Ruth, Bave — Boston — New York

DiMaggio, Joe — New York Americans — Yankees

Williams, Ted — Theodore — Boston

Martin, Billy — Phoenix — New York Yankees — Detroit

Mays, Willie — San Francisco

McCovey, Willie — WILLIE — San Francisco

Bat cards for players including Babe Ruth, Joe DiMaggio, Lou Gehrig, Pee Wee Reese, Ted Williams, Billy Martin, Yogi Berra, Mickey Mantle, Willie Mays, Willie McCovey, and Rod Carew were originally kept manually for every player, listing their orders and the players' selected bat specifications.

> "Hitting a baseball is the single most difficult thing to do in sport. It's the only field of endeavor where a man can succeed just three times out of 10 and be considered a great performer." —TED WILLIAMS

could be and spent time with the craftsmen who made Louisville Sluggers to understand how to maximize their potential. In fact, he once called his first visit to Hillerich & Bradsby's Louisville Slugger bat factory "...one of the greatest things I ever did in my life."

In the quest to find even the slightest edge against his competitors, Williams was known to climb over piles of wood billets at Hillerich & Bradsby's bat manufacturing facility, looking for any piece of lumber he thought held advantage over another. Here, he told a company craftsman, make my bat from *this*.

Quick hands, superlative hand-eye coordination, and endless hours in the batting cage were just not enough for this baseball perfectionist. Williams wanted the best tool of the trade he could find and was only half-joking when he said that after spending time with one of the craftsmen of the Louisville Slugger, he gave him $10 and instructions to save the best cuts of lumber for him.

"And I want to tell you," said Williams, "everybody said I got the best bats in the league."

Williams did little in his life halfway. If he set his sights on a goal, he gave it everything he had. The result of a lifetime pursuing excellence led Williams to the National Baseball Hall of Fame, the International Game Fish Association Hall of Fame, and the United States Marine Corps Sports Hall of Fame. He earned both the Presidential Medal of Freedom and two AL MVP Awards. His commendations as a fighter pilot in service of his country rival his long list of achievements as a Major League Baseball player.

Known by nicknames including "the Kid," "the Thumper," and "the Splendid Splinter," Williams is believed by some to be the greatest hitter who ever lived, while others say he was second to only Babe Ruth. Regardless, he was the last hitter to hit .400 in a season and won baseball's coveted Triple Crown twice, in 1942 and 1947. His 19-year career with the Boston Red Sox was twice interrupted by military service. After completing his naval training in 1942, he was waiting in San Francisco when VJ Day was declared and Williams soon returned

Major league players are particular not only about the length and weight of their bats, but often about the wood itself. Some players like a wide grain, others a more narrow grain, all thinking their preference produces a harder bat that is more difficult to break. In fact, the grain width makes little, if any, difference in the hardness of a high-quality piece of wood. On occasion, players who believe another player is receiving better bats will make some interesting orders. For example, after deciding that All-Star shortstop Barry Larkin was getting better wood in his bats than they were, his Cincinnati Reds teammates began ordering their bats under Larkin's name, thinking the craftsmen at Hillerich & Bradsby would be "fooled" into giving them better bats.

"I'd have been a .290 hitter without Louisville Slugger."
—TED WILLIAMS

Ted Williams was a frequent visitor to the Hillerich & Bradsby plant over the years.

Williams hit six game-winning home runs in his rookie year, including two grand slams.

home. His record-blazing career in baseball continued.

In 1952, the Korean War again interrupted Williams' baseball career. He flew 39 missions as a Marine pilot, many beside John Glenn, who has said that Williams was a "gung-ho" Marine. At least twice his jet was shot and badly damaged. Among his many military awards was the Navy Unit Commendation "for outstanding heroism against the enemy."

He returned to baseball right where he'd left it, hitting .345 in 1954, .356 in 1955, .345 in 1956, and defied his age in 1957, hitting a league-leading .388 with 38 home runs. He crowned this incredible run by winning Hillerich & Bradsby's Silver Bat Award in 1957 and again in 1958. Two years later, after announcing his retirement, Williams ended his career by batting .316 and hit a home run in his final at-bat.

Williams was also an everyday friend and neighbor to Junie Hillerich and family. When young Jack bruised his ribs, Junie Hillerich took him across the street to see Williams, who taped up his ribs like a professional sports trainer.

"I just remember I did not want to ever have to take the tape off," recalls Jack Hillerich. "I knew even then not every kid got the opportunity to be taped up by Ted Williams."

Junie Hillerich and Williams played golf together in Florida, using Hillerich & Bradsby's PowerBilt golf clubs. Other times, Williams was often in his garage, arranging and readying his fishing gear. Jack Hillerich remembers his father giving Williams some advice about fishing equipment.

"Ted said, 'Junie, you know a lot about golf and golf clubs, but you don't know a damn thing about fishing,'" says Hillerich.

"I was just like a young kid in a toy factory, 'cause I thought,
Boy, this is the greatest place I have ever been."
—TED WILLIAMS, DISCUSSING HIS FIRST VISIT TO THE HILLERICH & BRADSBY FACTORY

Ted Williams once complained about the way the handle tapered on his favorite bat. He sent them back, saying their grips didn't feel right.

Williams was right. Hillerich & Bradsby employees measured the grip with calipers against the models he had been using and discovered that Williams' new bats were $\frac{5}{1000}$th of an inch off. Williams could also discern differences in the weight of his bats. J.A. Hillerich Jr. once tested Williams by giving him six bats, five weighing exactly the same, the sixth weighing .5 ounces more. Williams correctly picked out the one with the seemingly imperceptible difference.

Every spring during his playing years, Williams would visit the Louisville Slugger plant. He would hardly break stride saying hello to executives in the office, but once with "his boys" in the factory, he called them by name and greeted them as old friends. Williams would soon be out of his coat and on a ladder, hand-picking timber for his bats.

Williams did respect Junie Hillerich's input on baseball issues, though. Jack Hillerich has the proof—a letter, now a family heirloom, that his father once wrote to Williams admonishing him for using bats that were too heavy. Williams was famous for using lightweight bats, whereas famous hitters before him, such as Ruth and Cobb, preferred heavier bats. Late one year, Williams opted for more weight and Hillerich believed the slowed swing was proving costly. The spring after the letter was written, Junie Hillerich prodded Williams again, telling his friend and neighbor to go back to lighter bats.

"You get more wood on the ball," Hillerich told Williams.

That season, Williams went back to ordering the lighter Louisville Slugger bats. He often told fellow players and fans about his belief in the benefits of a faster swing, generated from a light-weight Louisville Slugger.

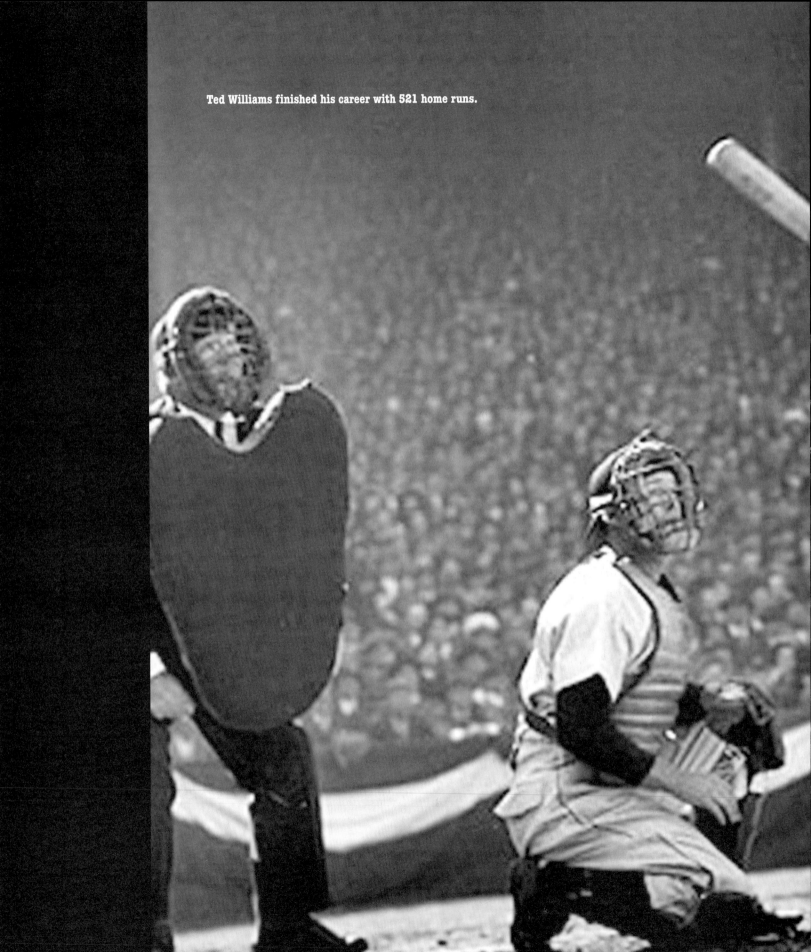
Ted Williams finished his career with 521 home runs.

Pee Wee Reese

Jackie Robinson deserves credit for the strength of character and courage he displayed—along with no small measure of athletic prowess—in breaking the Major League Baseball color barrier in 1947, but give teammate Pee Wee Reese credit for crushing the stereotype of the resentful white ballplayer.

One cannot discuss the career of these two great players without referring to the other. Dodgers pitcher Rex Barney once recalled Cincinnati fans at Crosley Field yelling at Jackie Robinson until Reese walked over and put his arm around the young Robinson, validating his presence and telling the world this man was his worthy teammate.

"You could have heard a gasp from the crowd," Barney said.

The beloved 5'10" Reese, who would captain the Dodgers throughout the 1950s, had refused to sign a player petition saying the team would not play for ownership if Robinson was signed. Robinson was signed, of course, and by the end of that year he was winning over the fans and fellow players as he hit 12 home runs on his way to winning the Rookie of the Year Award and helping the Dodgers win the National League pennant.

A native of Kentucky, the highly competitive Reese is said to have had a knack for the game of marbles as a kid, winning more than his share of "pee wees" (a type of marble) and earning him his nickname. As a 10-time All-Star shortstop, he led the Dodgers to seven pennants in 16 seasons and the only Brooklyn Dodgers World Series championship in 1955 (they would win five more World Series titles after moving to Los Angeles in 1958).

Reese and Robinson became recognized as one of the top double-play combinations in the history of the game. Not known for the long ball (126 homers in more than 8,000 at-bats), Reese became one of baseball's great leadoff hitters, winning top honors at various times for walks, stolen bases, and runs scored. But he was also known for clutch hitting and in 1954 hit a career-best .309.

Despite his success on the field, many know Reese best for his play-by-play broadcasts on CBS alongside Dizzy Dean in the 1960s, followed by a stint with Curt Gowdy in the late 1960s on NBC. He then joined Hillerich & Bradsby in 1970, working with the college and professional baseball staff to put the bat he loved in the hands of as many players as he could until his retirement in 1984. He is still remembered inside the company as one of the most loved and respected representatives in Louisville Slugger's 125-year history.

Harold Henry "Pee Wee" Reese was enshrined in the National Baseball Hall of Fame in 1984 and immortalized with a plaque that said he had "…intangible qualities of subtle leadership on and off the field, competitive fire and professional pride.…"

"When Jack entered [the major leagues], there were still a lot of people who didn't know if it was the right thing to do. Pee Wee used all of his leadership skills and sensitivity to bring the team together.… Pee Wee was more than a friend. Pee Wee was a good man." —RACHEL ROBINSON, JACKIE ROBINSON'S WIFE, IN *JET* (SEPTEMBER 13, 1999)

Hall of Fame shortstop Pee Wee Reese was a 10-time All-Star.

"Every home run that I hit in the major leagues was with a Louisville Slugger."

—HARMON KILLEBREW, 11-TIME ALL-STAR AND NINTH ON THE ALL-TIME HOME-RUN LIST WITH 573

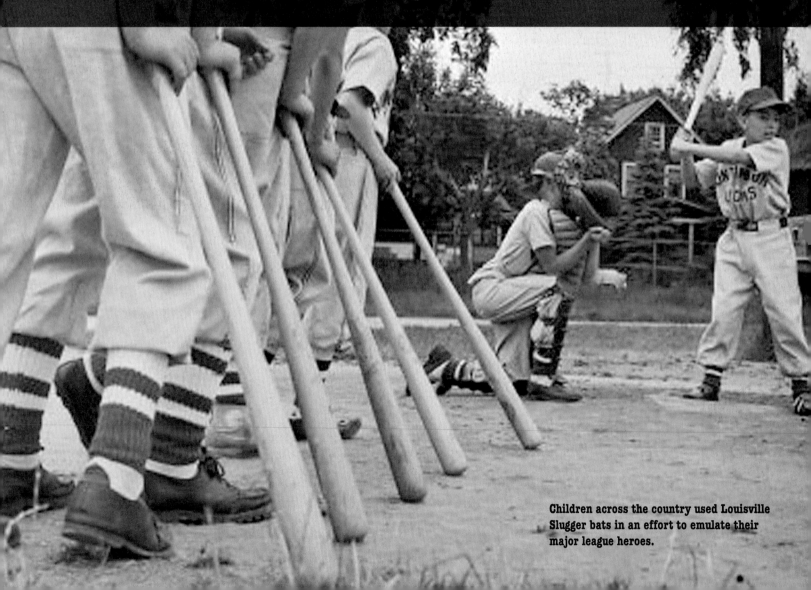

Children across the country used Louisville Slugger bats in an effort to emulate their major league heroes.

5

Building Upon Tradition

By the 1950s, Louisville Slugger had become the undeniable marketplace leader, providing personal service to all the best professional players as well as the opportunity for thousands of young amateur players participating in burgeoning youth leagues throughout the country to emulate the game's stars.

As one scribe wrote, Louisville Slugger made its "reputation in the big leagues" and its "profits in the youth leagues." In 1960, copies of the company's big-league bats sold in retail outlets for $4.60 each, while youth bats sold in much larger quantities fetched about $1.25 each. The big-league players under contract with Louisville Slugger got their bats from Hillerich & Bradsby, of course, along with any advice Junie Hillerich wanted to hand out.

For instance, when New York Yankees catcher Yogi Berra complained to the company that he was not getting enough pop out of his bats, Hillerich did some homework and discovered that Berra, a 15-time All-Star selection, was unconsciously turning the Louisville Slugger trademark on the bat toward the ball during his swing, hitting the ball against the grain and losing resiliency. Under the direction of the four employees still hand-turning custom bats at the time, a special order was made for Berra that featured the trademark running *with* the grain. When Berra made his habitual turn at the plate, he now found the sweet spot.

Lou Brock's Blast at the Polo Grounds

Blessed with speed, quick hands, and a personality that endeared him to St. Louis Cardinals fans and baseball fans across the country, Lou Brock was known throughout his 19-year Major League Baseball career more for his base stealing than for his power at the plate. The six-time All-Star, who amassed 3,023 hits and a .293 batting average in a career that spanned from 1961 to 1979, was always capable of hitting the long ball, however. He simply traded power to benefit his running game.

Although Brock retired from the Cardinals as baseball's all-time base-stealing leader, a record that stood until Rickey Henderson eclipsed it in 1991, he hit some memorable blasts swinging a Louisville Slugger. Brock often recalls one hit during his rookie season in 1962 when he played for the Chicago Cubs (he was traded to St. Louis in 1964). Only three players had ever hit home runs to center field at the old Polo Grounds in

New York after field and stadium reconstruction in 1923 left the fence a towering shot away, yet Brock delivered one of the blows.

"I got a hanging slider," said Brock, "a hanging curveball over my head. I chopped down on it, and the ball just took off."

The blazing Brock took off as well. The rookie rounded second base at full speed, glancing at umpire Bill Jackowski, who was signaling a home run. Brock took the signal to mean that if he ran as fast as he could, he might be able to log an inside-the-park home run. As it turned out, the ball had cleared the 20-foot-tall fence, which measured 460 feet from the base to home plate.

"And I never saw the ball go out," said Brock. "I came to the dugout and all of the Cubs were looking out to center field. [Ron] Santo said to me, 'Did you see that? Did you see that?' He's hitting me on the shoulder. He's really beating me up. 'Did you see that?'"

"Did I see what?"

"He said, 'The ball landed up there. It's way up there. No ball can land up there.'"

"They calculated it to be about 485 to 490 feet," said Brock. "And that was 1962. Based on inflation and the rate of growth, I think it is now 659 feet."

Lou Brock was a six-time NL All-Star.
Photo courtesy of AP Images

"This company has always been about
meeting the needs of the player.
My father learned what he did from his father."

—JACK HILLERICH

Keeping big-league hitters happy had been a core business philosophy since day one in 1884. Junie Hillerich and Frank Ryan, Louisville Slugger's professional player representative, were almost inseparable. They were determined to maintain the close relationships with the star players who had served the company well since the days of Honus Wagner and Ty Cobb. Ryan, says Jack Hillerich, would take *The Sporting News* and analyze every word in detail, collecting clips and articles on everything any big-league player did on the field and sending them to the players.

"He was almost like a switchboard," says Hillerich, "handling so much information and so many people. I have never seen anything like it."

The return of American servicemen to their wives led to the baby boom, which in turn led to a housing boom and tremendous industrial expansion designed to provide the household goods, cars, and other items that modern families were beginning to demand to fit their new, more active lifestyles—items that included sporting goods.

Domestic jet service began, and the interstate highway system was born in 1956 with the passage of the Federal Highway Act. American mobility was now unfettered. Television came of age, bringing news and sports into virtually every home. Kids could imagine themselves hitting a home run in Yankee Stadium as easily as they did in the sandlot down the street. With both time and money more abundant, the spectator sports grew. Everyone knew the names of people as diverse as Hank Aaron (baseball), Ben Hogan (golf), Althea Gibson (lawn tennis), and Wilt Chamberlain (basketball).

By the late-1950s, Henry Aaron had become a household name.

79

1954

HILLERICH &
BRADSBY BUYS A
LUMBER COMPANY
IN PENNSYLVANIA TO
ASSURE ITS SUPPLIES
OF NORTHERN WHITE
ASH

Baseball's popularity in America was about to be challenged the most by the rise of professional football, but you could not have convinced anyone at Hillerich & Bradsby of that fact. Louisville Slugger's popularity at the major league level, as well as in the rising sport of softball, drove the company's sales of wooden bats close to 5 million annually by 1960. Louisville Slugger was so popular, in fact, that the company was making more per year than its top two competitors combined.

Under Junie Hillerich's leadership, Hillerich & Bradsby had established a reputation for making the best bats used by the best baseball players in the world, and the company wanted to make sure it continued to protect its most precious commodity—the best wood available for making bats.

Quality of lumber, of course, makes all the difference when bat meets ball at high velocity. To create the perfect sweet spot, one that will send a pitched ball hurtling through an outfield gap or beyond a wall, a craftsman needs more than skilled hands and eyes and the right dimensions. First and foremost, he needs good wood to work with.

The company had already determined that northern white ash, typically found in the hills of New York and Pennsylvania and grown on the eastern and northern slopes, made the best bats, so Junie Hillerich purchased timber land and holdings in timber mills in those states, assuring Hillerich & Bradsby would not be left without needed lumber. To this very day, fifth-generation company leader John Hillerich IV (the son of Jack Hillerich and the great-grandson of Bud Hillerich), named CEO and president in 2001, says "It is all about the wood." Nothing has changed since grandfather Junie Hillerich bought hundreds of acres of white ash forest land in the 1950s and 1960s to make sure Louisville Slugger never lost its edge.

"First, you've got to find the right tree," says Hillerich. "Only one in 10 trees can make a great baseball bat." Only one in 20 makes a bat good enough for the major leagues. Hillerich estimates that it takes approximately 1 million pieces of wood to make 60,000 major league bats.

From there, selected logs are cut into billets, which face more culling for quality; in the end, about 5 percent of the wood cut is worthy of becoming a Major League Baseball bat. All cut wood is put to good use, of course, sold for various purposes when it does not reach the hands of players such as Derek Jeter and Evan Longoria, but this finite selection has long given Hillerich & Bradsby a distinct edge in making wooden bats.

"Nobody in the world can get as many good pieces of wood as we can," says John Hillerich IV. "Nobody. We have people in the sawmills who have worked there for 30 and 40 years who know what to look for. It made a difference for Ted Williams, and it makes a difference for any of the players we serve today."

NEW DIRECTIONS

Baseball bats were not the only growth area for Hillerich & Bradsby during the 1960s. Junie Hillerich recognized the rising popularity of golf, and the company's PowerBilt brand was expanded to meet demand. A young upstart named Jack Nicklaus was challenging the accomplishments of

Harmon Killebrew

With nicknames like "Hammerin' Harmon" and "Killer," Harmon Killebrew was known on the field as a fierce competitor with a powerful, compact swing at the plate. Standing 5'11" and weighing 210 pounds, Killebrew generated power with tremendous upper-body strength that helped him notch 573 career home runs.

Killebrew grew up in Idaho and was a standout baseball player and quarterback in high school who was offered a scholarship to play at the University of Oregon. Professional baseball scouts, including the Red Sox's Early Johnson, often visited Killebrew in high school, though in the end he got no signing offers.

"[Johnson] used to come down and visit me," said Killebrew. "And he said, 'If you ever get a contract offer [in baseball], please call me and see if the Red Sox can match it.'"

Harmon graduated from high school and turned down the scholarship offer to Oregon, playing semiprofessional baseball instead. He was paid another visit by Johnson, who delivered as a gift a Louisville Slugger model W166, the same model preferred by Ted Williams. As soon as he touched the bat, Killebrew was hooked.

"That just sold me on the Red Sox and Louisville Slugger," said Killebrew, who retired from baseball in 1975 after a 22-year career.

Killebrew was batting over .800 for the semi-professional team when Idaho senator Herman Welker told the Washington Senators' owner about the star player from his home state. The Senators made the 17-year-old Killebrew an offer. True to his word, Killebrew called Johnson to tell him the news

and to see if the Red Sox were still interested.

"I told him," said Killebrew, "and it was a bonus contract. It is laughable now, but they offered me $6,000 a year for three years, plus $4,000 a year for three years, which was the $12,000 bonus. And [Johnson] said, 'Well, you had better sign it, 'cause the Red Sox can't match that.'"

Killebrew became one of the American League's most feared hitters during the 1960s, crushing homers and driving in runs while keeping a quiet but admired and respected demeanor off the field. Throughout his career, he used the same brand of bat that he was introduced to by Earl Johnson.

"I always used a bat from [Louisville Slugger] and was proud of it," said Killebrew.

Harmon Killebrew knocked out 573 home runs during his Hall of Fame career.

As Louisville Slugger continued its dominance of the
baseball bat market, Junie Hillerich and his sons John
"Jack" III (center) and Hart (right) tour a yard full of
billets made from northern white ash in 1958.

all-time great Arnold Palmer, and advanced developments in equipment, such as the first two-piece balls, were allowing amateur and professional players alike unprecedented control and distance. The sport was gaining exposure and popularity on television, and easy trans-Atlantic travel by air made global stars of the world's best players.

Few golf clubs rivaled PowerBilt's Citation Persimmon Woods, which set the industry standard and were popular in Japan and throughout Asia. During the brand's professional sponsorship period and before metal driver and fairway woods came into favor, players using PowerBilt clubs won eight major championships—including Fuzzy Zoeller's victories at the 1979 Masters and 1984 U.S. Open—and more than 100 other professional events.

Junie Hillerich also led Hillerich & Bradsby to buy sporting goods company Wally Enterprises of Canada in 1966. Manufacturing croquet sets, billiard sets, and hockey sticks, Wally Enterprises primarily offered Hillerich & Bradsby entrance into the world of hockey, another major sport that relied on a wooden stick as its tool of the trade. Rebranding its hockey products as Louisville TPS (Tournament Players Series), the company expanded the line into retail outlets throughout the United States and Canada.

The addition of the hockey stick business, combined with the continued popularity of its wooden Louisville Slugger baseball bats and PowerBilt golf clubs, left Hillerich & Bradsby literally bursting at the seams in its aged downtown riverfront location. Junie Hillerich began to look for a new facility to meet future needs, but managing

existing operations was becoming more difficult. In the 1940s, manufacturing floor employees voted to join the United Steel Workers of America, and Hillerich & Bradsby's unionized employees went on strike in 1950 and again in the 1960s. With more than 400 employees manufacturing multiple products numbering in the millions, selling the family-controlled Hillerich & Bradsby suddenly seemed like a worthy option.

In 1965, Junie Hillerich struck a deal to sell the company, including its preeminent Louisville Slugger brand, to the sporting goods company AMF. Primarily a bowling company involved in equipment and facilities, the Virginia-based corporation was publicly traded and based the purchase price for Hillerich & Bradsby on its stock price. When the markets traded lower that year, AMF's share price dropped, and the company went back to Junie Hillerich wanting to renegotiate the sale price.

He declined.

At the time, Frank Bradsby's interest in the company was still held in a trust by St. Louis bankers. They felt Hillerich should have taken the lower price. After the deal was off, they sold Bradsby's shares back into the company.

Later in the 1960s, Junie Hillerich was diagnosed with cancer. His oldest son, Jack, was the heir apparent, but he was only in his twenties. Believing it was in the family's best interest, Junie Hillerich negotiated a sale for Hillerich & Bradsby once again, this time to a privately held company. He was spending time at his Sarasota home in early January 1969 when a deal was all but done—final negotiations were being made

1959

HILLERICH & BRADSBY PRODUCES ITS 100 MILLIONTH LOUISVILLE SLUGGER BAT

1966

HOCKEY STICKS ARE ADDED TO THE HILLERICH & BRADSBY PRODUCT LINE

1969

JOHN JR. DIES AND
HIS 28-YEAR-OLD
SON, JOHN A. "JACK"
HILLERICH III, TAKES
THE LEADERSHIP
ROLE

**John A. "Jack"
Hillerich III was only
28 years old when he
took over leadership
of Hillerich & Bradsby
following the death of
his father.**

over $500,000 in the sale price. But Junie Hillerich died before the final deal was completed, and Hillerich & Bradsby remained a family business as it neared the final decade of its first century in business.

ANOTHER HILLERICH TAKES CHARGE

When Jack Hillerich was born in 1940, flowers flooded his mother's Louisville hospital room. The oldest son born to that generation of the family, it was widely expected that Jack would one day inherit leadership of Hillerich & Bradsby.

As a youngster, Jack grew up in Louisville playing sandlot baseball, and the family business thrilled friends by providing some unique bats to swing in games. Hillerich could have grabbed any new bat from the factory to bring to the field, but he and his friends preferred using some of the broken big-league bats that found their way back to the company. Jack would pick some out, patch the wooden bats back together again with nails and tape, and bring them to games to the delight of peers. The youngsters played, taking labored cuts with the same oversized bats used by the best baseball players in the world, trying to emulate the stances and swings of their idols and hoping a little of their magic might rub off them.

"That's what I could bring to the table," Hillerich says.

Hillerich eventually left Louisville for four years, attending college at Vanderbilt. In the summertime, he came home from college and worked for Hillerich & Bradsby, gaining experience as a company apprentice. Upon graduating from Vanderbilt with a degree in business in 1961, Hillerich went to work immediately at the family-controlled company. He considered other opportunities for experience first, but one prospective employer advised him that because everyone knew where he would end up, he might as well start there.

When he started out working in the company's timber yards in the Northeast, Hillerich & Bradsby did not even have a forklift, instead handling 6 million pieces of lumber by hand, piling them into a wagon that was pulled down the street from the lumberyard to the factory by a farm tractor. Employees had it down to an exact science,

Moving bats out of the Hillerich & Bradsby factory
has been modernized decade by decade.

Jack Hillerich needed only to look in a display case full of commemorative Louisville Slugger bats to understand the importance of his company to the game of baseball.

Jack says. The process worked, but it required 55 employees to get the job done.

Jack figured they could do it more efficiently, and his brother-in-law's textile business and its "pile of scrap seat belts" gave Hillerich an idea. He made a rack from the seat belts, filled it up with billets, and picked it up with a forklift.

"The wood plant manager, Charlie Quick, told me, 'It won't work. The forklift won't make the grade,'" Hillerich says with a smile. "I knew I had him them, because it was flat."

Of course, the billets spilled everywhere on the first try.

"If I was not the president's son," he recalls, "I would have been gone."

———————————●———————————

Ralph Garr played in the International League before he won the National League batting championship in 1974. One day he came to Louisville for a game but had forgotten his bat. Garr stopped at Hillerich & Bradsby's factory for another. Employees checked his specifications, produced the bat, and sent it to the ballpark. In the end, Garr refused to use the bat, which had been made precisely according to his specifications, because the bat makers didn't have time to brand it with his signature.

The invention needed improvement, so Hillerich tinkered with it until the process was perfected, drastically improving efficiency and allowing one man to now handle the work of 55.

Jack Hillerich's next assignment was working for 18 months under Frank Ryan, the sales manager in charge of Louisville Slugger's professional bats. In that role, Jack learned how the company met the needs of the game's best players by paying attention to even the smallest details.

When his father died in 1969 and left Hillerich & Bradsby in his hands at the age of 28, Jack Hillerich remembers more than a few people wondering if he could run the company at such a young age. There was no question, however, that he had the right genes for the job. The grandson of Bud Hillerich had seen his grandfather's dedication firsthand as a young child.

"I remember seeing him," Jack Hillerich says. "His hair was white, looked like he had cotton on top of his head. And I remember he was pretty domineering. I used to look at these letters he wrote to employees, leaving very specific details on what not to do."

For two generations, Bud Hillerich and sons Ward and John were frequent visitors in baseball clubhouses across the country. But when leadership passed to Jack Hillerich, he returned to focusing on the finer points of woodworking that so intrigued his grandfather in the 1880s.

"I did not feel comfortable in the clubhouse the way they did," Jack Hillerich says. "I got the gene from my grandfather…the love of manufacturing. Bradsby was the original marketing guru.

Catcher Johnny Bench spent all 17 of his big-league seasons with the Cincinnati Reds.

Johnny Bench

Most professional baseball players say being in the major leagues was a childhood dream, yet few can trace their inspiration back as far as former Cincinnati Reds catcher Johnny Bench, considered one of the best to ever play his position.

From his earliest memories, Bench says his father hoped his son would become a big-league ballplayer. Bench's father had shown promise as a catcher, but military service interrupted his dream, relegating him to semiprofessional baseball. So when young Johnny and his brothers began to play at a early age in rural Oklahoma, his father let them know that becoming a professional baseball player was not only possible, it was reasonably attainable. Breaking into the big leagues as a catcher was the easiest route, he said.

In the small town of Binger, Oklahoma, population 661, Bench found baseball to be among the best ways to spend his time. His school did not have a football or soccer team; it was just baseball and basketball.

"There certainly were not a lot of diversions," said Bench. "So we played baseball."

In the second grade, Bench remembers his teacher asking students what they wanted to be when they grew up.

"Ronnie said he wanted to be an insurance salesman, and Dennis and Robert wanted to run the dairy, and Sharon wanted to be a teacher, and I said, 'I want to be a Major League Baseball player,' and everybody laughed," Bench said.

A popular game among Bench and his two older brothers involved a home-run derby, played with a wooden bat and "an old evaporated-milk can." When they had enough for a full baseball game, Bench and his brothers and friends tacked broken wooden bats back together, keeping repairs in place with tape, and had a game, almost every day, regardless of the elements. Sometimes, Bench's father would play in games pieced together in open lots buffered by cropland.

"Dad would hit the ball so far, I mean, it would go in the corn field," he said.

Bench says his teacher asked students again in the eighth grade what they wanted to be, and students still laughed when he repeated his dream of making it to the big leagues. He was big for his age in junior high school but says he did not "have much else to go with it." He grew by his junior year, though, and at 6'0" and 180 pounds with a big swing, a strong arm, and uncanny instincts, professional scouts began visiting Oklahoma and classmates stopped laughing at Bench's dream.

The rest is history, of course, considering Bench was drafted by the Reds in the second round in 1965 and reached the big leagues in 1967. He was a 14-time All-Star selection who won two World Series rings and hit 389 home runs before retiring in 1983 as perhaps the best catcher to ever play the game. Bench was elected to the National Baseball Hall of Fame in 1989.

He sold them, and my grandfather made them. I came along in the 'make' mode. I like to see new ideas and find a way to make it work."

But Jack Hillerich undersells his impact on Louisville Slugger's marketing and building of the brand. In the early 1970s, Hillerich was barely settled into an executive role when he decided the company should drop the name Hillerich & Bradsby from its bats, focusing solely on the Louisville Slugger logo. That was the company's stronghold trademark, and that was the brand that would lead the company forward in its second century of business. He says that move may be his greatest lasting impact on the company.

Not all decisions have worked out that way, Hillerich admits. For example, just after his father died, his mother's house was littered with trunks full of seemingly valueless memorabilia. Baseball collectibles were not lucrative at the time, and the company had been so deeply involved in the game for so many years, items such as old World Series game programs, notes from meetings, used bats, and personal notes from players seemed to be just taking up space. Jack Hillerich's mother did not want them. Company employee Jack McGrath did, however, and claimed them for himself (although the Hillerichs' family silver set was, of course, returned as soon as it was found).

On another occasion, the company was faced with disposing of a storage shed filled with unused Louisville Slugger bats. Two employees wanted the bats and eventually sold them to eager collectors for thousands of dollars. Jack Hillerich used to half-jokingly ask his friends how well they made out with the memorabilia in those trunks and the bats from the shed. Their responses were usually, "Jack, you don't want to know!"

Hillerich tells these self-deprecating stories for the sake of humor and history, but under his leadership the Louisville Slugger brand not only survived into a second century of business, —a rare feat for a family-owned company—it thrived, transitioning from a throwback icon into a contemporary corporation with annual revenue exceeding $100 million.

A MOVE ACROSS THE RIVER

Among the bigger decisions made and faced by Jack Hillerich came in the late 1970s, when the company's aged downtown Louisville facilities were in need of an upgrade. A unionized factory, some employees feared Hillerich & Bradsby might follow competitors and move south, finding new and cheaper workers. In the 1960s, the company had bought property near Pinehurst, North Carolina, and considered moving its golf manufacturing business there; in the end, Junie Hillerich changed his mind, not wanting to leave the company's workers behind. Jack Hillerich shared the sentiment and did not want to get away from the company's core strength—a specialized, skilled workforce based in the Louisville area.

But when faced with the company's outdated facility, Hillerich was forced to consider the availability of a new, bargain-priced plant available just across the river in Indiana. Built for a piano company that never opened, the site had everything Hillerich & Bradsby needed. A new, vacant building on 30 acres of land with access to a railroad spur seemed like the perfect place for a company making close to 7 million wooden bats each year. Hillerich kept the decision to move across the river into Indiana quiet; only four people inside the company knew, he says.

Hillerich was just 32 years old, still fresh out of business school. So when he took Hillerich & Bradsby employee Jack McGrath to lunch to tell him the company was moving out of downtown Louisville, he got an unexpected response.

"[McGrath] said, 'Oh my god! Do you know what you are doing?' That is when it hit me."

The next day, the company arranged for buses to carry Hillerich & Bradsby employees across the river to show them the plant. Nothing like the brick and crumbling mortar structure the company had occupied since its founding, the new 65,000-square-foot building had it all, save for a Louisville address. The space seemed perfect for ushering the company into its next successful era.

George Brett retired in 1993 after collecting 3,154 hits during his 21-year major league career.

"Never, never once did I use any other bat but Louisville Slugger."

—GEORGE BRETT, HALL OF FAMER AND A CAREER .305 HITTER FOR THE KANSAS CITY ROYALS

6

Challenges of a New Era

Baseball had changed considerably since gaining popularity in the mid-1800s, but the bat itself had remained mostly the same, made from wood within length and weight specifications. The arrival of the 1970s would alter both the bat and the game at the amateur level at once, however, and welcomed the arrival of wood's fierce competitor—aluminum.

In its new factory, Hillerich & Bradsby was running at full capacity. Baseball was at its peak of popularity and it showed no signs of diminishing. Youth leagues flourished. In metropolitan areas like New York and Los Angeles, inner-city children and teenagers migrated to the game as an escape from the mounting racial and economic tensions that surrounded them. Teaming together in 1974 at Los Angeles' Locke High School, two young players—Eddie Murray and Ozzie Smith—exemplified the movement that saw baseball serve as an outlet for many African American players.

Eddie Murray was one of 12 children, including four brothers who played baseball professionally at some level. Growing up in the Watts neighborhood of Los Angeles, baseball was a diversion from an era filled with racial tension. Almost every day he and his brothers, sisters, and neighborhood friends participated in a pickup game of sandlot baseball, and few could rival his talent as a teen.

Dusty Baker's Three Keys to Hitting a Baseball

A player wanting to hit the baseball needs a good bat, of course. But when he or she stands in at the plate against competitive pitchers, it takes more than desire and a good bat to be the best, says former player and successful Major League Baseball manager Dusty Baker.

In a playing career including stints with four teams from 1968 to 1986, Baker knocked in more than 1,000 runs as a professional, with a career batting average of .278 and two Silver Slugger Awards to his credit. As a manager for teams including the San Francisco Giants, Chicago Cubs, and currently the Cincinnati Reds, Baker has been known as a player's coach, sharing his experience from years in the game. His advice when it comes to hitting is simple: focus on concentration, homework, and practice to improve your chances for success at the plate.

Considering even the best hitters fail 70 percent of the time they come to bat in a game, Baker says concentration is the key for all players. If you cannot see the ball, says Baker, it will be hard to hit. Concentration makes the ball look bigger.

"If you don't see the ball by the time it leaves the pitcher's hand and you don't pick it up until halfway, then you are susceptible to being behind on fastballs and being ahead on breaking stuff or off-speed stuff," Baker said. "So concentration is No. 1."

Good hitters must also do their homework. Concentrating on every pitch is key, but it also helps when players have studied pitchers and know their tendencies. If a hitter understands what or where a pitcher might throw, concentration is more focused. Back in the day, Baker says, players had to have a "computer in their brain." Now, however, the computer and frequent television broadcasts make it easier for players to study.

"You have to know the repertoire of pitches a guy has, and you should know the sequence he likes to throw them in," said Baker.

Finally, all good hitters must spend an extraordinary amount of time with a bat in hand, seeing live pitched balls. Baker says the best hitters, from Ted Williams to Tony Gwynn, spend the most time in the batting cage, seeing an array of pitches over and over again.

"You don't have long to recognize the difference between a sinker, fastball, and breaking ball," said Baker. "The more you see [in practice], the more your reactions get sharper, and it goes directly from your brain to your body and how you react. This is why practice and repetition are so important."

When Ozzie Smith and Eddie Murray played together as seniors in high school, Murray was the standout. He batted .500 and was selected in the third round of the 1973 Major League Baseball draft, debuting just four years later in the big leagues with the Baltimore Orioles. Murray hit the ground running, winning the AL Rookie of the Year Award (.283 batting average, 27 home runs, and 88 RBIs) while swinging Louisville Slugger bats. Murray later retired as one of baseball's all-time greatest switch-hitters, accumulating more than 3,200 hits in a career highlighted by eight All-Star selections and three World Series appearances. Upon his induction into the National Baseball Hall of Fame, he thanked his youth coach for teaching him the fundamentals and a love for the game at a young age.

Born in Mobile, Alabama, Ozzie Smith's family moved to Los Angeles when he was six years old. Smith's father was a truck driver and his mother was employed in a nursing home. When they worked and he was out of school, Smith was playing baseball or basketball at the local YMCA or working on his reflexes by bouncing a ball off the steps in front of his home. He remembers sleeping on the floor as a 10-year-old during the infamous Watts riots of 1965; he also recalls taking city buses to 25 or more Los Angeles Dodgers games every year as a teenager, dreaming about one day being a big-league player himself.

Smith can also remember himself, Murray, and their fellow teammates coming into contact for the first time with an all-new baseball product, the aluminum bat. Too heavy to comfortably wield and too expensive for the Watts team to stock, the bat made a peculiar ping upon striking the ball but also seemed to have a much larger sweet spot. Even a good miss, says Smith, traveled well.

For Murray, the path to the big leagues seemed to be a foregone conclusion, and he quickly left the aluminum bat behind. Smith, on the other hand, was an all-around athlete good at both basketball and baseball but without obvious professional baseball characteristics. Undrafted out of high school, Smith went to a small college in California on a baseball scholarship, walking onto the baseball team in 1974—the same year the NCAA approved the use of aluminum bats.

Ozzie Smith played at Cal State Polytech University just as aluminum bats began to gain popularity.
Photo courtesy of Getty Images

Smith says he recognized even then that the amateur game would never again be the same.

A superlative fielder known for his remarkable hand-eye coordination, Smith learned to become a switch hitter in college using an aluminum bat. Setting a school base-stealing record, his offensive feistiness and creativity combined with his sure glove and wide range to make him a professional prospect. He was originally drafted in 1976, then signed a contract when drafted a second time in 1977 with the San Diego Padres. He was traded to St. Louis in 1981 and blossomed into a 15-time All-Star selection at shortstop. Smith never again played with an aluminum bat in competition after his senior season in college, collecting more than 2,400 hits with Louisville Slugger wooden bats in the majors.

SLOW TO REACT

As Hillerich & Bradsby looked to expand its production capacity, baseball was quietly changing on the amateur level faster than a young Jack Hillerich or others closely associated with the game imagined possible. For decades, Louisville Slugger had been one of a very select few baseball bats in consideration for use by players of all ages and skill levels. The wood was impeccable, the craftsmanship unequaled. However, wooden bats could not compete with the baseball world's new wonder material.

A tannery in the small town of Tullahoma, Tennessee, that specialized in making leather-covered baseballs and softballs under the trade name of Worth decided to produce its first bat in 1970, made not from wood but aluminum. After graduating from Vanderbilt in 1959, John Parish went to work at Lannom Manufacturing Company, a company owned by his father and the maker of Worth products. John talked his father into entering the baseball bat business in 1970, and he believed the company's only chance for success in an industry dominated by Louisville Slugger was with an entirely different product.

The metal baseball bat was first patented in the 1920s, but players never warmed to it and it was never produced on a large scale. But when Worth first took its aluminum youth bat to market, individual players and organizations including Little League quickly adopted the new technology, preferring the cost effectiveness thanks to the bats' durability. The early versions of the aluminum bat were heavy and clunky and did not hit the ball farther than wooden bats, but they did not break. The familiar crack of the bat once heard on youth ballfields was being replaced with a ping, causing baseball purists such as Jack Hillerich and many Louisville Slugger employees to cringe.

Hillerich & Bradsby began selling its own aluminum bat right after Worth made its first, but the company did it as an afterthought. One serious player went so far as to call the Louisville Slugger aluminum bat a toy, and nobody at Hillerich & Bradsby disputed the slight.

Baseball was a traditional game, and tradition for more than a century was about the wooden bat. Besides, when you are making and selling some 7 million wooden bats per year, imagining the market will shrink by 80 percent in a matter of just a few years might have been difficult.

Unfortunately for Hillerich & Bradsby, however, that is exactly what happened. Little League approved the aluminum bat in 1971 and college baseball did the same in 1974, the year Louisville Slugger's production peaked. At first, nobody thought wooden bats would be eradicated at the amateur level; aluminum was immediately popular but not immediately better. Thus, the company maintained its emphasis on wood quality and precision craftsmanship, making and selling some aluminum bats at lower retail prices just to join the burgeoning party.

While Hillerich & Bradsby sat on the sideline in the race to make the next generation aluminum bat, a family-owned California company specializing in producing metal archery arrows was making progress in metal bat technology. Easton originally produced a private-label aluminum bat on par with others in the market but was working behind the scenes to develop a superior product. Engineers found a way to make the metal bat's walls thinner while maintaining its strength and curved shape. Reduced weight gave Easton's metal bats a decided edge in distance and power over wooden bats.

In the mid-1970s, Easton launched its own bat products, sending a loud and clear message to Hillerich & Bradsby. Wooden bat sales dropped almost overnight from the peak production of 7 million per year to just 1 million. Luckily, Major League Baseball did not approve the use of metal bats, sticking with wood for competitive and safety reasons.

The amateur game was on a decidedly different path, however. No longer was price an issue; players of all ages would pay any price for the lightest, latest, greatest aluminum bat that turned .290 hitters into .330 hitters, made doubles leaders home-run leaders, and transformed powerless players unable to wield heavier bats into feared sluggers.

While Louisville Slugger tried to keep the price of its metal and wooden bats down, Easton doubled prices on its new technology aluminum bats, and buyers in both baseball and softball scooped them up. Also, an Easton engineer in the late 1970s developed an aluminum hockey stick that gained approval from the National Hockey League.

"Easton was a real savvy competitor," recalls Jack Hillerich. "They were just beating the pants off of us."

Adding further insult to injury, a fledgling California manufacturer named Taylor Made introduced metal drivers and fairway woods and was quickly followed by other competitors, including Calloway, drastically altering golf club sales for Hillerich & Bradsby.

Almost overnight, the view from the big facility named "Slugger Park" located in Jeffersonville, Indiana, had turned gloomy. The company was slow to react to the explosion of aluminum bats because it believed in wood. The trend was undeniable, though, and in 1978 Hillerich & Bradsby purchased Alcoa's California manufacturing facility, which made Louisville Slugger aluminum bats under a private-label agreement. Jack Hillerich recalls not wanting to buy the factory because the price was too high but remembers being told that if Hillerich & Bradsby did not buy it, Alcoa would just "burn it down."

1973

CRAMPED FACILITIES CAUSE THE COMPANY TO MOVE GOLF CLUB MANUFACTURING ACROSS THE RIVER TO JEFFERSONVILLE, INDIANA, AND BAT-MAKING SOON FOLLOWS

1974

HENRY LOUIS "HAMMERIN' HANK" AARON BREAKS RUTH'S CAREER HOME-RUN RECORD; THE NCAA LEGALIZES ALUMINUM BATS AND FOREVER CHANGES COLLEGE BASEBALL

97

After being introduced on a wide scale in the mid-1970s, aluminum bats quickly became the preferred bat throughout college baseball and softball. Today many bats such as this Catalyst2 employ composite materials such as graphite, fiberglass, and resin that are lighter and stronger than aluminum.

Hillerich made the deal, and the company entered the metal bat–manufacturing business. Still, Hillerich & Bradsby sold aluminum bats as more of a cost-conscious discount model, rather than as a premium, marketplace leader. The company specialized in wood and was not sure how to make an aluminum bat popular. With lacking technology, it even tried painting an aluminum bat yellow to make it look like a wooden bat, but the product did not sell very well.

From 1980 to 1985, company profits dropped by 90 percent and the sales growth experienced almost every year since the 1800s came to a complete halt. Job layoffs followed. Hillerich & Bradsby held tightly onto the wonderful Louisville Slugger brand, still preferred by virtually all of the professional baseball players, but the company's long-running strategy of building a reputation in the big leagues and earning profits in the little leagues was in jeopardy.

Although he had been in the leadership role at Hillerich & Bradsby for 15 years, Jack Hillerich says he had not fully taken charge of the company. Often, he looked to another senior employee, Bill Becker, for advice, particularly in regard to how Hillerich & Bradsby should react or adapt to the evolving games its products supported. Hillerich admits that when his father died, Becker should have become president of the company; he just didn't have the right last name. For years, Hillerich turned to Becker for advice. At one point, a company board member asked Hillerich, "Just who's running this company?"

Jack Hillerich took the point to heart, taking a more aggressive and proactive role with firmer decision-making. He knew something had to be done; allowing the company to dwindle was not an option. Louisville Slugger, a brand founded by his grandfather and great-grandfather, would not go down on his watch. In a conversation about his responsibility to run the company, Hillerich talked about writing himself a note when he first became CEO. It was a reminder to make sure he didn't risk everything, to not "bet the farm."

To change Hillerich & Bradsby's fortunes in the face of a threat bigger than the fire of 1911 or the flood of 1937, Hillerich took a cue from his heritage and turned to the one group that had always provided the right answers.

GO TO THE SOURCE

With the company facing difficult odds and his family's long-standing business heritage on the line, Jack Hillerich had to foster change within the organization. The company was resting on its well-earned laurels from the previous century, but the games of amateur baseball and softball demanded more than reputation. These were the 1980s, when the influence of affluence was at an all-time peak. Twenty million people went to the movies every week. Average salaries reached almost $16,000 for the first time. Players wanted lighter bats with ball-crunching power and the status that the "Me Generation" craved, and money was no object.

"I'd been taught to keep the price down," Hillerich said. "We'd sell a $15 Fence Buster, and Easton would sell a $50 bat."

Hillerich got the message loud and clear when he traveled to a leading softball tournament

1978

HILLERICH & BRADSBY BUYS OUT ALCOA'S ALUMINUM BAT COMPANY IN CALIFORNIA, WHICH HAD BEEN MAKING ITS BATS SINCE 1970

Steve Garvey

When Steve Garvey grew up in Tampa, Florida, in the 1950s and 1960s, he considered himself the luckiest young man in the world because he got to serve as a bat boy during spring training for the Brooklyn Dodgers, New York Yankees, and the Detroit Tigers. Before he was a bat boy, however, Garvey got an up-close-and-personal view of a baseball team behind the scenes, forming a lasting memory.

Garvey's father drove the bus for the Dodgers during spring training in 1956. His father had come home on a Thursday night asking if his seven-year-old son had any tests in school the next day. When told no, the elder Garvey told his son they were going to pick up the Brooklyn Dodgers at Tampa International Airport and take the team to St. Petersburg to play an exhibition game against the Cardinals.

"The next morning, we picked up the bus, and we drove to the tarmac…and the plane pulled up," recalled Garvey. "The door opened and off came Walter Alston and then Pee Wee Reese and Gil Hodges and Carl Furillo and [Carl] Erskine, [Roy] Campanella, and all the 'Boys of Summer.'"

Garvey said he stood off to the side, and each of the Dodgers patted him on the head as they walked by. Later that day, he carried around their heavy wooden bats, and Hodges played catch with him before a game the Dodgers won 5–3. At home that night, the starstruck young Garvey could not get to sleep.

"Dad," he said. "There's this smell. I can't figure it out, and it is keeping me up."

"I know what it is," his father said.

"What?"

"It's pine tar," his father said. "You will probably never forget that smell the rest of your life."

His father was right, of course, as Garvey went on to play for the Los Angeles Dodgers and the San Diego Padres from 1969 to 1987. As a Dodger,

Garvey was considered one of baseball's finest young players. The 10-time All-Star first baseman lives in lore, though, for a feat accomplished in 1984, his second season with the Padres.

Facing the Chicago Cubs in the National League Championship Series, the Padres were facing elimination and were deadlocked in the bottom of the ninth inning of Game 4 in a 5–5 tie at San Diego's Jack Murphy Stadium. Strong-armed Cubs closer Lee Smith was on the mound, but San Diego's Tony Gwynn reached base on a single with one out. Garvey then came to the plate, launching a 370-foot walk-off home run to right-center field, ending the game and crushing the hopes of Chicago, a franchise that had not appeared in the postseason since 1945.

Garvey was sure he would be a hated man in Chicago following the home run, considered the deciding blow in a series won by San Diego, but he did not take into account reaction from Chicago White Sox fans.

"I would walk down the street [in Chicago] and somebody would yell from the other side, 'Way to go, Garv! You beat the Cubs!' And then a Cub fan would boo me. But that's baseball, you know? Baseball has tremendous fans, and they are usually territorial and regional."

Playing the Cubs the very next season at Wrigley Field, Garvey says he got a full dose of fan treatment during his first at-bat. Facing pitcher Rick Sutcliffe, the crowd rose to its feet when Garvey stepped to the plate with boos and taunting chants. Garvey stepped back and tipped his hat, inciting the crowd even more. Then, he promptly tripled to right-center field, quieting the crowd.

What happened the next time Garvey came to the plate?

"I got knocked down," said Garvey. "But that was back in the good old days. They don't do that anymore."

Steve Garvey finished his career one hit shy of 2,600. *Photo courtesy of AP Images*

Hillerich & Bradsby improved its aluminum bat technology by working closely with softball players.

held annually in the South for top teams from throughout the region. He watched from close behind the backstop as every player walked to the plate, taking cuts with an Easton or Worth bat—but no Louisville Sluggers. Not one. Hillerich & Bradsby was still doing large volume business, selling its lower-priced aluminum bats to discount retailers by the thousands, but the products did not match the company's well-established, high-quality wooden bat brand.

"Our metal bats were just dime-store bats," he says, recalling the epiphany. "They were no good."

Louisville Slugger had served the top players for a century, but now the top amateur players wanted bats made by other companies at twice the price. Louisville Slugger was selling its aluminum bats to discount retailers for $19.95 each and million-dollar orders made for good volume, but the brand would not last long that way. Outside of its wooden bat business at the professional level, Louisville Slugger was no longer listening to the

customer. The company had lost touch with its most important core value—serving the player's needs.

Hillerich knew something had to be done but was not sure what. When approached by the owner of a Georgia "Super Slowpitch" softball team with a large fan following about sponsorship, Hillerich listened.

Based in Gordon, Georgia, Gary Hargis' Elite Coatings team was one of the nation's best in the Independent Softball Association in the early 1980s, packing standing-room-only crowds at games and winning with some of the flashiest, farthest-hitting players in the game. These players were bigger than life in most of the smaller communities where they played on weekends, the same way baseball players like Babe Ruth and Ted Williams were bigger than life in the cities they had played in years before.

Hargis wanted to make a run at a national championship, and he needed money to get better players, including Bill Gatti, a Louisville native who, standing 6'6" and weighing 285 pounds, hit 312 home runs during the 1983 season, and Craig Elliott, who hit 390 home runs the same year in 142 games. Hargis made Jack Hillerich an offer: for the sum of $40,000, Louisville Slugger could sponsor Elite Coatings. The offer was intriguing. Hillerich knew well of Gatti, a former University of Louisville football player known locally as the Louisville Slugger because he could hit the softball "a mile."

Still, Hillerich initially balked at the offer.

"We can't do that," he said. "Too much money."

Jack Hillerich teamed with Elite Coatings to help Louisville Slugger gain a foothold in the aluminum bat market.

"Come watch us play," said Hargis. "You will see."

Hillerich had never been to a Super Slowpitch softball tournament before, but he went to the Smoky Mountain Classic in Maryville, Tennessee, to see Hargis' team play. Immediately, Hillerich was struck with the realization that Hargis was offering a bargain. Every time an Elite Coatings player came to the plate, fans knew his name and the brand and specifications of the bat he swung.

Jack Hillerich wrote Hargis a sponsorship check on the spot.

Back in Louisville, Jack Hillerich told members of the company's leadership team he had cut a $40,000 sponsorship check to a softball team from Georgia. Naturally, everyone thought Hillerich had momentarily lost his mind. Hillerich & Bradsby was facing hard times, and giving $40,000 to a seemingly obscure softball team was a risky venture. But Hillerich was convinced he was onto something valuable. Louisville Slugger built its reputation by finding out what the best players wanted and needed and then giving it to them. By sponsoring Elite Coatings, the company

George Brett

In the 1960s and early 1970s, the windows facing the backyard of the Brett family home in El Segundo, California, were under constant threat from baseballs. The four brothers in the Brett family were spread out in age, but they shared one thing—a love for baseball.

"We played a lot of ball in the backyard," said George Brett, "and I'm sure we had Louisville Sluggers back then."

All four Brett boys made it to professional baseball—Bobby and John to the minor leagues, and Ken and the youngest brother, George, to the major leagues, where they combined to play for 35 years. Ken made it first as a big leaguer, drafted as a pitcher at age 17 by the Red Sox (George was 12 at the time). Ken passed away in 2003, but he still holds the record as the youngest pitcher to ever appear in a World Series.

George would not only become the star of the family, but also one of the greatest players in all of baseball. Playing his entire 21-year career with the Kansas City Royals, George Brett set numerous batting records, garnering a mantle full of trophies and honors. Hitting a career .305, he also notched 3,154 hits and 317 home runs. When George Brett's plaque was hung in the National Baseball Hall of Fame in 1999, it proclaimed him to be a "clutch hitter whose profound respect for the game led to universal reverence."

By the time Brett played his last game in 1993, he had employed numerous models of bats, including the famed Louisville Slugger R43 that was made for Babe Ruth. His favorite was said to be a Louisville Slugger T85. Brett has stated, "Never, never once did I use any other bat but Louisville Slugger."

Some best remember Brett for the infamous pine tar incident. Hillerich & Bradsby subsequently worked with Brett in an effort to make light of the controversial incident, creating a miniature bat named the "George Brett Pine Tar Special," which quickly became a collector's item.

Brett was named the AL Most Valuable Player in 1980, the year he won his first Silver Slugger award from Hillerich & Bradsby.

"George Brett could get
good wood on an aspirin."

—JIM FREY, FORMER KANSAS CITY ROYALS MANAGER

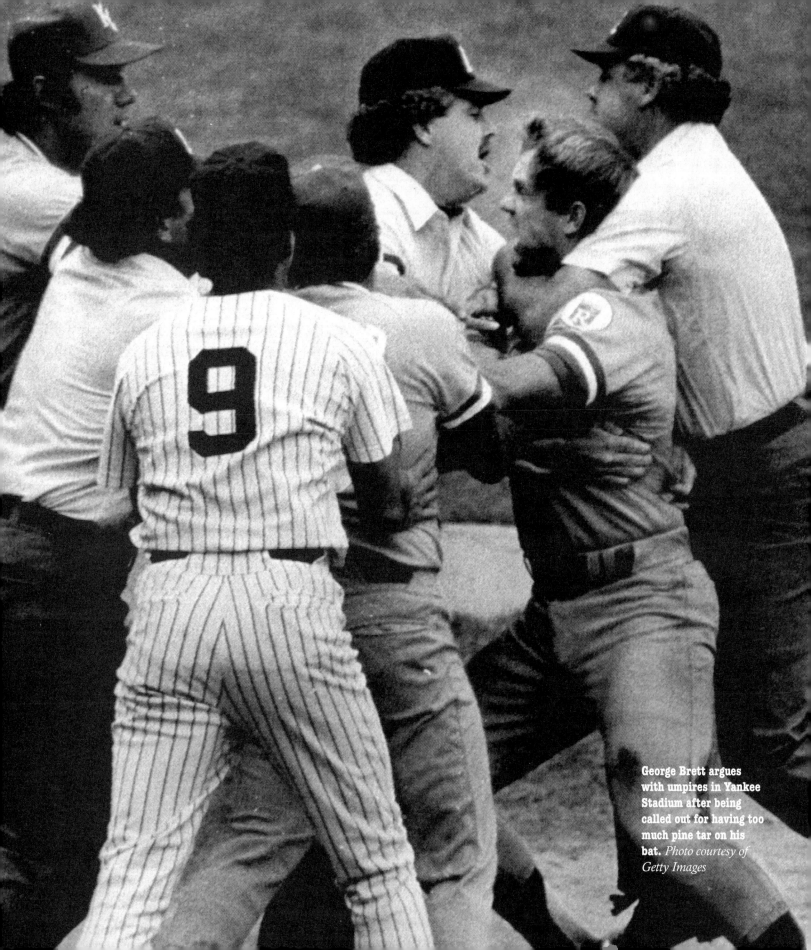

George Brett argues with umpires in Yankee Stadium after being called out for having too much pine tar on his bat. *Photo courtesy of Getty Images*

1990

GEORGE BRETT
BECOMES THE FIRST
SILVER BAT WINNER
TO WIN THE AWARD
IN THREE DECADES
(1976, 1980, 1990)

could receive frank feedback resulting in a better aluminum bat.

"I said to myself, 'I have to do this,'" Jack Hillerich said. "Forty thousand dollars was a lot of money, but it was not going to break us or bring down the company. I had to try. We had to do something." He refers to writing that check as a "magical moment" in his career.

Jack Hillerich and team worked with Hargis and Elite Coatings team members the way his grandfather and great-grandfather worked with the first professional baseball players, seeking input in relation to weight, feel, and hitting dynamics. But the first bat they handed the team was given right back, with the players saying it was not good enough. Hargis said, "Put your logo on an Easton and bring that to us." As Jack Hillerich explains, "If they didn't believe in the bat, they couldn't win."

The company began working intensively on making a better aluminum bat with direct input from Elite Coatings team members, making the most finite adjustments in an effort to build the perfect aluminum bat, one that could match the same quality and excellence as Louisville Slugger's wooden bats had for a century. The process took two years and thousands of dollars in research, but Hillerich & Bradsby got it right, giving Elite Coatings and amateur baseball and softball players a product worthy of its brand.

"It was a turning point for us," recalls Jack Hillerich. "We just drew upon our history. We did not build a model and give it to Ted Williams. Ted told us what he wanted. The Elite Coatings softball team told us, 'This does not feel right,' and we went back to work until it did feel right. Once we

got it, we were back into our element, serving the best players with the best products."

LOUISVILLE SLUGGER IN THE SPOTLIGHT

While Hillerich & Bradsby refocused its efforts in the aluminum bat business, its famous wooden bats were still capable of making headlines of their own.

A 13-time All-Star selection, George Brett was well established by 1980 as one of the best hitters in all of baseball. A third baseman for the Kansas City Royals, Brett led his team into the World Series that year against the Philadelphia Phillies after batting .390 for the season and winning the AL Most Valuable Player Award. He had a superlative series against the Phillies, hitting .375, though the Royals lost in six games.

Despite his accomplishments, Brett is perhaps best remembered for a moment that occurred several years later and would become known as the "pine tar incident."

The date was July 24, 1983, and the Royals were in New York playing their perrenial rivals, the Yankees. With his team trailing 4–3, Brett had just slugged a two-run home run in the top of the ninth inning off famed relief pitcher Rich "Goose" Gossage when he was called out by umpire Tim McClelland. It was decided that the pine tar on Brett's Louisville Slugger bat extended more than 18 inches from the handle, a violation of Major League Baseball rules.

Because Brett's hitting techniques were so consistent and precise, he often got more uses out of a wooden bat than most big-league players, and because Brett did not wear a batting glove, he used pine tar on his hands to improve his grip on the bat. Brett had been using the same bat for weeks that season, and he had handled it so often that the pine tar extended 24 inches up the bat.

The seeds of the incident were planted weeks before while New York was playing in Kansas City. Yankees third baseman Graig Nettles noticed Brett's bat and told manager Billy Martin about it, who did not say a word until Brett's home run in New York. When Brett hit the ball, he customarily dropped his bat next to home plate, and Martin quickly notified McClelland of the extended pine tar.

Realizing he was being called out because of the pine tar, Brett charged from the dugout in an arm-waving frenzy. The antics got Brett ejected from the game and made headlines on nearly every television network from coast to coast. The Yankees won the game 4–3, but the Royals protested the result to American League president Lee MacPhail, who ordered the game be resumed at a later date. MacPhail said bats with too much pine tar should be removed from the game but that Brett hadn't violated the "spirit of the rules."

The famous game was concluded later that season, and the Royals won the official contest 5–4. The pine tar–coated Louisville Slugger bat was originally sold to a collector for $25,000, but Brett later bought it back for the same amount, plus the gift of another valuable souvenir. The bat now rests in Cooperstown as part of baseball's Hall of Fame exhibit.

WHO SAYS ALUMINUM ISN'T A PRECIOUS METAL?

"The formula for our success is having a really good product. You cannot fool good hitters with anything less than the best."

—MARTY ARCHER, PRESIDENT OF LOUISVILLE SLUGGER

Colleges across the country have made it clear they want their bats to feature the latest technology, and after some initial struggles, Hillerich & Bradsby is now a leader in the market.

CHAPTER 7

Return to Louisville

By the 1990s, Hillerich & Bradsby was not only back in the game at all levels, its bats were among the best hitters could find in any category, including wood, aluminum, professional, amateur, or youth. In returning to its heritage of building only the best products with the top players in mind, Hillerich & Bradsby reinforced Louisville Slugger's performance-oriented reputation, launching a new standard in its second century of baseball service.

Advanced technology became expected as a part of every facet of life during the last decade of the 20th century. The birth of the Internet fostered the use of personal computers in homes coast to coast. New technologies changed the way people thought about automobiles, the way they communicated, and even the way they watched sports on television. Why should expectations for bat-making technology be any lower?

Among the company's earliest innovations in aluminum bats was making the handle easier to grip; other developments included a range of designs from weighted ends and pressurized air chambers inside bat barrels to thinner bats made from strong alloy metals. Hillerich & Bradsby's SpringSteel, for example, features uniquely coiled steel on the interior, while the launch of the first Air Attack was an homage to Nike's popular line of athletic shoes.

The inspiration for the Air Attack was Marty Archer, a Hillerich & Bradsby employee for three decades. Archer, now president of the Louisville Slugger division of Hillerich & Bradsby, grew up in Louisville's Shawnee Park neighborhood on the city's west end during the late 1950s and early 1960s when "baseball was it." He remembers his mother coming to wake him every morning in 1961 with updates of the Mickey Mantle–Roger Maris home-run battle and running down professional scores from the day before. Shawnee Park had 18 baseball diamonds for youth and amateurs, and games in the summertime went on all day and all night long.

When older players left the park at night, broken wooden bats were often discarded. Archer and his friends often scavenged for the bats early the next day, repairing them for play with penny nails and tape. Naturally, the bats usually carried the Louisville Slugger label. The sandlot relationship and the understanding that the best players in baseball used the homemade product was the extent of Archer's knowledge about the branded bat, but that was enough to make him proud.

"Growing up," Archer says, "there were three things that made me really proud of Louisville. One was native Cassius Clay, who later became Muhammad Ali. The second was the Kentucky Derby and Churchill Downs. The third was Louisville Slugger. To know players like Mickey Mantle played with Louisville Sluggers in the big leagues just made my year."

When given the opportunity to work at Hillerich & Bradsby in the 1970s after working for several years in manufacturing with another company, Archer didn't hesitate. He loved baseball and the Louisville Slugger brand, and he loved what Jack Hillerich told him about the business when they first met. "He always talked about stewardship," Archer recalled. "He was never about making as much money as he possibly could. He considered this legacy a gift. Jack did not want us to focus on being No. 1. He wanted us to focus on giving players the best product possible."

Archer says Jack Hillerich's commitment to building a better aluminum bat came at the same time he focused on building a better business, implementing Total Quality Management principles throughout the workplace. Doors came off offices, and dialogue between the top office floor and the factory floor improved. Jack Hillerich, a Deming Institute trustee, was always known for

Marty Archer, president, Louisville Slugger Division. When Jack Hillerich was asked how Hillerich & Bradsby remained successful for so long, he said, "We've found many Marty Archers."

spending most of his time at the office near the factory floor. He loves the smell of sawdust and gets excited talking about a new lathe. "When he's into something," says Archer, "he's really into it."

When they became confident with metal technologies, Hillerich & Bradsby applied creative strengths from years of bat-making experience to finding solutions and at times were amazed themselves by the results. Employees had a seemingly endless supply of ideas about making a better bat and shared the information during brainstorming sessions with engineers, who implemented the best into design and production. For example, one day Archer had walked into a meeting in the early 1990s holding one of his new Nike Air shoes. Buffering the foot with an air compartment cushion, the shoe was in inspiration for Archer. "How about if we try this?" Archer asked, holding up the shoe. The concept was developed and became a popular bat for the company, which marketed the Louisville Slugger amateur bats under the TPX (baseball) and TPS (softball) series.

Wood at Louisville Slugger would always be king, of course, because of Hillerich & Bradsby's heritage and core strength. Several dozen wooden bat manufacturers still exist, yet Louisville Slugger commands more than 60 percent of the professional baseball business because of its product and legacy. The company believes that a .300 hitter with the latest, best metal bat would likely become a .200 hitter in an instant if forced to switch to a wooden bat, but nobody at Hillerich & Bradsby wants to lose any part of baseball's illustrious history with the wooden bat.

A GRASSROOTS MOVEMENT

To get its new aluminum bats into the hands of the best players in amateur baseball, Louisville Slugger devised a strategy similar to its professional baseball strategy, which started more than 100 years before when Pete Browning signed his first endorsement contract. But college players cannot accept endorsement fees or any other type of incentive, so the company devised a parallel strategy that would not violate any NCAA regulations. Creating an advisory board in the early 1990s, the company negotiated with dozens of the top coaches in college baseball and softball the same way Nike negotiated a decade before with basketball coaches.

Having top-level endorsers, including coaches from leading programs like Florida State, Rice, and Texas, would put the bats in the hands of those players most admired by even younger players. Because the majors played with wood, younger players using aluminum bats

During his brief flirtation with baseball, Michael Jordan's bats were in as much demand as his basketball memorabilia. The first shipment of Louisville Slugger bats featuring Jordan's name and "Chicago White Sox" on the barrel disappeared en route to training camp in the spring of 1994 and never turned up. Another order of Jordan's M216 bats was shipped to replace them.

Tony Gwynn

Baseball players and coaches at all levels have many different theories on the best way to get a hit, but one strategy most hear or share at one time or another relates to the benefits of swinging the bat early on a pitch.

Tony Gwynn, however, had a different strategy. A 15-time All-Star and seven-time Silver Slugger Award winner, Gwynn retired after 20 seasons with the San Diego Padres with a .338 career batting average. Using a Louisville Slugger Model B276C, which measured 33 inches and weighed just 30.5 ounces, Gwynn was a rare contact hitter in the home-run age of baseball, adept at hitting to all fields and never batting below .309 in a full season.

Gwynn's secret as a hitter was seeing the ball first, swinging late second. By getting the ball back as far as possible into the hitting zone, Gwynn found more time to swing the bat.

"Most hitters flip that theory around," said Gwynn. "Instead of hitting the ball at the back of the plate, they want to hit the ball out in front. But when you hit the ball out in front, you've got less time to do what you set out to do."

Taking more time to identify pitches was compensated for with a lighter bat, which allowed Gwynn to get wood on the ball more quickly once the decision to swing was made.

"To hit the ball out in front, you have got to be pretty pure consistently," Gwynn said, "but you do not have to be as pure when you back the ball up to the plate. When I back the ball up to almost even with the plate, I know I'm going to be successful. I know there is not a guy in this league who can just flat-out throw the ball by me."

Giving himself more time to see the ball at the plate worked well for Gwynn, elected in 2007 to the National Baseball Hall of Fame after retiring with 3,141 career base hits and striking out just 434 times in 9,288 big-league at-bats.

Tony Gwynn visited with Jack Hillerich during a tour of the Hillerich & Bradsby factory.

"Performance is the only thing that matters. It's all about the top player."

—JACK HILLERICH

began looking to the college ranks for their role models. The College World Series held in Omaha—where it's been growing in size and scope since the first game there in 1950—has become nearly as big to those players wanting the best aluminum bat as the World Series had been to the generation growing up with Louisville Slugger's wooden bats in the 1950s and 1960s. More than 80 college baseball coaches and programs were signed up with Louisville Slugger's TPX bats in the 1990s, helping company sales begin steady growth. The strategy was to reconnect with the company's history in supplying the top players and to showcase the success of hitters with Louisville Slugger TPX bats in their hands.

Some years, bat sales grew as much as 20 percent from the lowest period in the 1980s. Louisville Slugger's timing was perfect, considering performance-level aluminum bat sales experienced phenomenal growth in the 1990s, increasing 70 percent from the decade before.

Nobody minded that some bats cost $200 or more because they offered a much larger sweet spot. In college baseball, batting averages soared. The aluminum bats caused some concern for the safety of pitchers, but the game's popularity increased, drawing crowds from the West Coast to the South and turning the sport into a revenue producer for many schools. In no time, Hillerich & Bradsby's Louisville Slugger competed with Easton head-to-head in the metal bat business, while maintaining its industry-leading position in wooden bats. Thus, despite a sagging golf business—Hillerich & Bradsby did not adapt to metal technologies in its PowerBilt golf clubs as quickly

The Stanford Cardinal are among the many college baseball teams that swing Louisville Slugger TPX bats.

as it did with baseball bats—the company was soaring once again as sales were passing $100 million annually.

A HITTER'S GAME

College baseball bats were not the only ones coming to life in the 1990s. Slugging had increasingly become a part of Major League Baseball with each passing season, and in an America where bigger was better, home-run hitters stole the show. In the auto industry, the oversized SUV was en vogue, and in the stock market, the stock of any company with ".com" in its name soared. In baseball, the home run was all that seemed to matter, and fans had plenty of long-ball excitement.

STIFFNESS AND STRENG

THE EXOGRID CONCEPT IS SIMPLE:
INCREASE HANDLE STIFFNESS AND STRENGTH WITHOUT INCREASING WEIGHT.

CARBON COMPOSITE INSERTS
Metal is trimmed in a grid pattern, then replaced with carbon composite inserts that are several times stronger and lighter than the metal they replace.

EXCLUSIVE EXOGRID BI/FUSION™ PROCESS
Using a combination of heat and extreme pressure, the sleeve, inserts and metal wall are bonded to function as a single, solid unit.

EXOGRID®
TECHNOLOGY

Exogrid and Bi/Fusion™ are registered trademarks of TyaiTek Sports.

A new dimension in performance technology.

CB9X *EXOGRID®*

LENGTH	WEIGHT
31"	28 oz.
32"	29 oz.
33"	30 oz.
34"	31 oz.

Packed 1 per carton

- ST+20 alloy/composite hybrid
- 2 5/8" barrel, -3 oz. without grip
- Patented Pro Cup® end cap
- Synthetic grip, 31/32" tapered handle
- Meets college and high school BESR bat standards

Stiff is good.
Stiffer is even better.

The last thing you want at the moment of contact is for your bat handle to flex. When the handle flexes, the barrel can't. That reduces your trampoline effect. A stiff handle produces more barrel flex, resulting in maximum trampoline effect and, ultimately, greater performance.

The Exogrid is among the latest developments in bat technology, using carbon composite inserts to create handle stiffness and greater trampoline effect.

CARBON COMPOSITE SLEEVE
of the Exogrid is the carbon sleeve, ...ides greater handle stiffness than ...alone ever could. Unidirectional ...he full length of the handle.

SL9X *EXOGRID*®

LENGTH	WEIGHT	
28"	19.5 oz.	• ST+20 alloy/composite hybrid
29"	20.5 oz.	• 2 5/8" barrel
30"	21.5 oz.	• Patented Pro Cup® end cap
31"	22.5 oz.	• Synthetic grip, 7/8" standard handle
32"	23.5 oz.	
Packed 1 per carton		

YB9X *EXOGRID*®

LENGTH	WEIGHT	
28"	16.5 oz.	• ST+20 alloy/composite hybrid
29"	17.5 oz.	• 2 1/4" barrel
30"	18.5 oz.	• Patented Pro Cup® end cap
31"	19.5 oz.	• Synthetic grip, 7/8" standard handle
32"	20.5 oz.	
Packed 1 per carton		

Louisville Slugger® TPX

TRITON 3X COMPOSITE

EXTREME

The unique 3-piece design of Triton allows the barrel and handle to be designed and built as individual units. The transition bubble area brings everything together to function as a more advanced 1-piece bat.

THE BUBBLE TRANSITION ZONE adds strength to the handle and transition area.

The handle is made even stiffer and stronger with the addition of the Bubble Transition Zone.

The Bubble Transition optimizes the relationship between the barrel and handle, making a stiffer and stronger bat.

Our exclusive computer-designed pattern precisely positions the angles of graphite layers, resulting in an extra-long barrel with a huge sweet spot and outstanding performance.

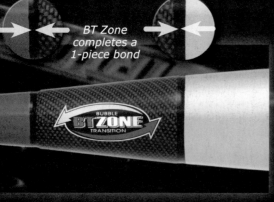

BT Zone completes a 1-piece bond

BT Zone functions as the bonding of the barrel and handle and provides a stiffer handle and transition.

-3

CB91T *TRITON*

LENGTH	WEIGHT
31"	28 oz.
32"	29 oz.
33"	30 oz.
34"	31 oz.

Packed 1 per carton

- 3X 3-piece composite design
- Bubble transition zone
- 2 5/8" barrel, -3 oz. without grip
- Synthetic grip, 31/32" tapered handle
- Louisville Slugger® end cap
- Meets college and high school BESR bat standards

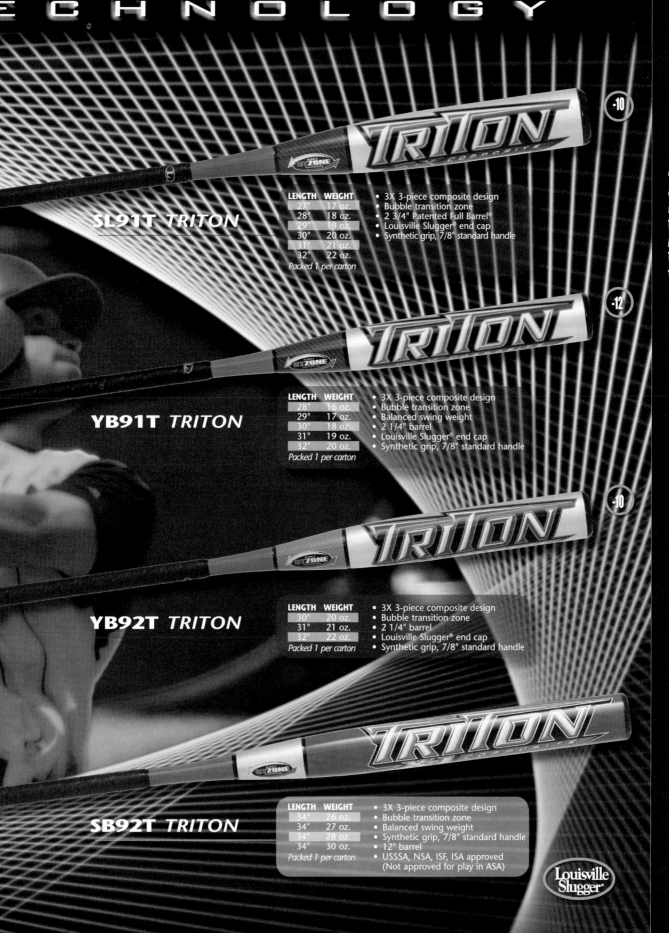

The Triton bat combines three sections into one bat with layers of graphite inside the barrel to enlarge the sweet spot.

SL91T *TRITON*

LENGTH	WEIGHT
27"	17 oz.
28"	18 oz.
29"	19 oz.
30"	20 oz.
31"	21 oz.
32"	22 oz.

Packed 1 per carton

- 3X 3-piece composite design
- Bubble transition zone
- 2 3/4" Patented Full Barrel®
- Louisville Slugger® end cap
- Synthetic grip, 7/8" standard handle

YB91T *TRITON*

LENGTH	WEIGHT
28"	16 oz.
29"	17 oz.
30"	18 oz.
31"	19 oz.
32"	20 oz.

Packed 1 per carton

- 3X 3-piece composite design
- Bubble transition zone
- Balanced swing weight
- 2 1/4" barrel
- Louisville Slugger® end cap
- Synthetic grip, 7/8" standard handle

YB92T *TRITON*

LENGTH	WEIGHT
30"	20 oz.
31"	21 oz.
32"	22 oz.

Packed 1 per carton

- 3X 3-piece composite design
- Bubble transition zone
- 2 1/4" barrel
- Louisville Slugger® end cap
- Synthetic grip, 7/8" standard handle

SB92T *TRITON*

LENGTH	WEIGHT
34"	26 oz.
34"	27 oz.
34"	28 oz.
34"	30 oz.

Packed 1 per carton

- 3X 3-piece composite design
- Bubble transition zone
- Balanced swing weight
- Synthetic grip, 7/8" standard handle
- 12" barrel
- USSSA, NSA, ISF, ISA approved
  (Not approved for play in ASA)

Louisville Slugger®

BUILDING OFF THE SUCCESS OF EXOGRID, H2 TECHNOLOGY IS THE NEXT STEP IN OPTIMIZING THE COMPOSITE/ALLOY HYBRID DESIGN.

1-PIECE DESIGN

The exclusive H2 design bonds the ST+20 barrel the 3X composite seamlessly, providing the outstanding performance of a 1-piece stiff handle design.

3X COMPOSITE

ST+20

STIFFER HANDLE/TRANSITION

The H2 design utilizes a full 3X composite handle and transition area. The move to a full 100% graphite composite design in the transition allows for an even stiffer handle than offered in Exogrid. Graphite is lighter and stronger than aluminum, allowing for a stiffer handle.

STRENGTH / TOUGHNESS

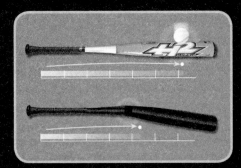

A stiff handle produces more barrel flex, resulting in maximum trampoline effect and, ultimately, greater performance.

THE BARREL SECTION OF H2 *is constructed with the industry leading ST+20. Its outstanding strength and toughness provide the performance, feel and sound that top players demand. A lighter handle/transition means a longer barrel and sweet spot.*

9H2 *HYBRID* -3

LENGTH	WEIGHT
31"	28 oz.
32"	29 oz.
33"	30 oz.
34"	31 oz.

Packed 1 per carton

- ST+20 alloy/3X composite hybrid design
- 2 5/8" barrel, -3 oz. without grip
- Patented Pro Cup® end cap
- Synthetic grip, 31/32" tapered handle
- Meets college and high school BESR bat standards

9H2 *HYBRID* -8

LENGTH	WEIGHT
27"	19 oz.
28"	20 oz.
29"	21 oz.
30"	22 oz.
31"	23 oz.
32"	24 oz.

Packed 1 per carton

- ST+20 alloy/3X composite hybrid design
- 2 5/8" barrel
- Patented Pro Cup® end cap
- Synthetic grip, 7/8" tapered handle

The H2 combines a high-tech aluminum alloy with composite materials for a one-piece bat designed for strength.

9H2 *HYBRID* -12

LENGTH	WEIGHT
28"	16 oz.
29"	17 oz.
30"	18 oz.
31"	19 oz.
32"	20 oz.

Packed 1 per carton

- ST+20 alloy/3X composite hybrid design
- 2 1/4" barrel
- Patented Pro Cup® end cap
- Synthetic grip, 7/8" standard handle

Hillerich & Bradsby worked with Alcoa to test and develop the latest bat technology using Alcoa's new aluminum alloys. ST+20 was developed exclusively for Louisville Slugger bats to provide the strongest alloy available on the bat market.

EXCLUSIVE NEW BAT ALLOY UNVEILED

America's #1 Aluminum Manufacturer Teams Up With America's #1 Bat Maker

LOUISVILLE – In a recent announcement that has captured the attention of the sporting goods industry, Alcoa and Louisville Slugger jointly introduced GEN1X™, the strongest alloy ever developed for an aluminum bat. This unprecedented move marks the first time that Alcoa has developed an alloy exclusively for a single bat manufacturer.

The impressive GEN1X alloy exceeds 100 ksi (the measurement of an alloy's strength). Unlike anything on the market today, GEN1X is the most technologically advanced aluminum bat alloy Alcoa has ever developed.

Through a development process that spanned several years, Alcoa research and development engineers formulated a breakthrough combination of aluminum, zinc, copper, zirconium, magnesium and traces of titanium to obtain GEN1X's incredible strength.

In aluminum bat construction, an alloy's "yield strength" is key to bat design, performance and durability. Engineers feel that the yield strength of GEN1X will give Louisville Slugger a solid advantage in all aspects of bat design.

According to sources at Louisville Slugger, the GEN1X alloy has opened the door to a whole new world of design possibilities. The strength of this new alloy enables Louisville Slugger engineers to design bats with the ultimate combination of balance, wall thickness, performance and durability. Many experts believe GEN1X bats will quickly become the standard by which all others will be judged.

The first bat to employ the GEN1X alloy has been appropriately named "GEN1X." Already, this bat has had tremendous success on the field and is rapidly gaining the attention of batters throughout the country.

Louisville Slugger, based in is the world's leading bat manufacturer. The company has been making bats since 1884, making Louisville Slugger one of the oldest and most respected names in the game. In fact, \ the company has been around almost as long as the game itself, providing quality bats to players at all levels of the game.

Alcoa is the world's number one supplier of alumi bat tubing. Accordi Alcoa enginee with the chemi

ALLOY STRENGTH		
GEN1X	100+	
Scandium XS	96.3	
C555	92.0	
C405 PLUS	89.7	
CU31	81.3	

ALCOA

Louisville Slugger®

TP·X® -3OZ

GEN1X

BESR CERTIFIED

bat manufacturer. The company has been bats since

The Rise of Fast-Pitch Softball

Baseball may have started primarily as a men's game in the 1880s, but eventually women found a home and heroes of their own on slow- and fast-pitch softball diamonds across the country. The sport has been around for decades, played in summer leagues and by high school and college teams, yet it was not until the 1996 Olympic Games were played in Atlanta that fast-pitch women's softball exploded nationally and inspired participation from coast to coast.

Naturally, Louisville Slugger was there, praoviding high-performance bats for high-performance players just as it had for so many years with baseball and men's softball. In 1996, no star was bigger on the world stage than Dot Richardson, a former UCLA women's basketball player and softball standout who wanted to be an astronaut, a singer, or an actress as a child but found her place in fast-pitch softball captaining and leading the American team to the 1996 gold medal with a game-winning home run.

The drama, combined with increased opportunities for college scholarships, increased the popularity of the sport and led to young women taking up the game in competitive youth leagues throughout the country. Richardson, who ultimately fulfilled one of her childhood ambitions by becoming a physician, led the United States to another gold medal in 2000, became a signature star for Hillerich & Bradsby's Louisville Slugger softball bats

in the same way Honus Wagner represented wooden bats a century before.

Endorsing models such as Louisville Slugger's FP21 Dr. Dot Richardson and the FP19 Dot Richardson TPS, Richardson has become a leading name in fast-pitch softball. Her fellow UCLA alumnus, Lisa Fernandez, is the "No. 1 softball player in the world," according to Richardson. Fernandez endorsed models including the FP18 Lisa Fernandez Air Attack 3 and the FP203 GEN IX Lisa Fernandez.

A WORD FOR THOSE WHO AREN'T AFRAID TO DREAM

Almost everything worthwhile in life begins with a dream. And for over 100 years, thousands of athletes like Dot Richardson and Lisa Fernandez have reached their dreams with Louisville Slugger.

Hillerich & Bradsby's TPS series of aluminum bats were used by the 1996 gold medal-winning U.S. Olympic softball team.

Ken Griffey Jr., the son of former professional standout Ken Griffey, possesses one of the smoothest and most fluid swings baseball has ever known. In 1997, he won the AL Most Valuable Player Award, hitting 56 home runs for the Seattle Mariners while posting a .304 batting average with 147 RBIs. A Louisville Slugger signature player throughout his career, Griffey used the popular Louisville Slugger C271 model, favored in the 1970s by former Chicago Cubs outfielder José Cardenal.

St. Louis' Mark McGwire, who was named AL Rookie of the Year with Oakland in 1987 after hitting most of his 49 home runs with a Louisville Slugger, hit 70 home runs in 1998, outdueling the Cubs' Sammy Sosa's 66 homers to set a then–Major League Baseball single-season record. The home-run barrage continued into the new millennium, as San Francisco Giants outfielder Barry Bonds broke the single-season home-run record in 2001 with 73.

Home runs soared among many players in the game, causing fans and pundits to wonder if juiced bats or baseballs had anything to do with increased home-run production. Louisville Slugger, for its part, was making the same quality bats according to league specifications that it had delivered since the beginning.

History would later reveal that an indefinable number of players, including pitchers and hitters alike, relied upon performance-enhancing drugs to build strength and endurance, but such peripheral issues of the game do not involve Louisville Slugger. Making the best bats possible is all the company is about. Record books are for others to debate.

Bonds' feat was accomplished using a maple bat; Hillerich & Bradsby had previously determined that maple did not make for the best bats, but as Bonds' tear that season gained momentum, more professional players strong enough to swing maple bats sought them out. True to its tradition of meeting players' needs as long as they fit within the rules of baseball, Louisville Slugger upped its maple bat production over the following years.

Making maple bats is easier today than it was 100 years ago, thanks to new wood kilns that remove moisture from maple logs, reducing their weight and improving their strength. As maple bats gained in popularity throughout the professional ranks, Major League Baseball commissioner Bud Selig expressed growing concern in 2008 over shattering maple bats some said split with more force than ash bats.

Lenny Dykstra was one of many major league players who were very particular about their bats. For example, Dykstra sent back the special bats he got as the National League Championship Series began in 1993. To commemorate the postseason, Dykstra's Louisville Slugger bats were stamped "1993 NLCS" under his signature. But the Phillies outfielder balked, saying that he wanted his bats for the series to be exactly the same as the ones he used all season—with "Philadelphia Phillies" stamped under his name. The bats were, of course, replaced.

Ken Griffey Jr.

When Ken Griffey Jr. landed in Cincinnati in 2000 after an 11-year career with Seattle, few doubted he would destroy Major League Baseball's all-time home-run record. After all, he'd already logged 398 homers, including an average of more than 50 per year for the past four seasons. He was being mentioned in the same sentence with Babe Ruth.

Hank Aaron himself dubbed Griffey Jr. as the man most likely to break the record. Looking back, perhaps the bone he broke in his finger during his rookie year in 1989 was foreshadowing the rest of his career. At the time of the injury, he was leading all major league rookies with a .289 average and had slammed 13 home runs and knocked in 45 RBIs. His production dropped after the injury, however, and he finished third in the Rookie of the Year voting.

But his credentials were in order when he arrived to play for the Reds a decade later. He'd grown up watching his father Ken Griffey Sr. play for the Reds during the Big Red Machine era of the mid-1970s. Griffey Jr. was building his own résumé: back-to-back 56-home run seasons in 1997 and 1998. Four American League home-run titles. Winning the MVP in 1997 and finishing in the top 20 an impressive nine times. Winning Hillerich & Bradsby's Silver Slugger Award seven times in the 1990s.

Then a series of bizarre injuries—most resulting from his own hustle in the field and on the base paths—plagued Griffey for the next seven years, robbing him of what should have been some of his most productive years at the plate. It began with a hamstring injury in 2000 that slowed him throughout the 2001 season. In 2002, a rundown left him with a torn patella tendon in his right knee. In 2003, he suffered season-ending surgery for an ankle injury and had shoulder surgery after dislocating it diving for a ball. In 2004, he tore his hamstring sliding in the outfield and continued to be slowed throughout 2005. In 2006, he dislocated a toe jumping into the wall for a fly ball and was diagnosed with very painful pleurisy in 2007.

Despite these obstacles, Griffey Jr. continues to hammer out home runs between stints on the disabled list and currently is fifth on the career home-run list with 611. Simple math suggests that if he'd hit for four more years in the early 2000s like he did the previous five years, he would easily be over 750. Through it all, he stuck with his Louisville Slugger C271.

"[My father] let me experiment with everything. From Cooper, Adirondack, to some other bat that was made, and it all came back to Louisville [Slugger]," Griffey Jr. said.

His father was always partial to Louisville Slugger. "The first bats I ever played with in Little League, Pony League, were Louisville Slugger," Griffey Sr. said.

Traded in 2008 to the White Sox, Griffey Jr. has logged 2,680 career hits and 1,612 runs as he heads back to Seattle in 2009. True fans will also remember him for his towering shot in the 1993 Home Run Derby, when he became the first and only man to hit the B&O Warehouse behind the right-field wall of Baltimore's Oriole Park at Camden Yards, measured at 460 feet. Despite his injuries, Ken Griffey Jr. has been one of the most prolific hitters ever in the game and an all-time Louisville Slugger great, both on and off the playing field.

"We'd go to Yankee Stadium and take batting practice
in the tunnel. When he was 13 or 14, I threw everything
but the kitchen sink and I couldn't strike him out.
I knew I had something special."

—KEN GRIFFEY SR., THREE-TIME ALL-STAR, ON HIS SON'S BASEBALL PROWESS

The popularity of Louisville Slugger maple bats increased dramatically after Barry Bonds used one to set a new home-run record in 2001.

"We don't make the rules of baseball.
We serve the needs of the players and the game
by giving them the best bat they can find."

—JACK HILLERICH

"Maple tends to break in two, and what you see is half of the bat flying across the infield," said Chuck Schupp, Hillerich & Bradsby's director of professional sales. "Ash tends to splinter or flake. It's not always visible from the stands, and a hitter may not realize it's cracked until he gets back to the dugout and looks at it."

Louisville Slugger is admittedly not a proponent of the maple bats, deciding decades ago that white ash served baseball best. But Louisville Slugger will gladly produce maple as long as players want them and they fit within professional baseball's rules, and by 2005 almost half of the wooden bats Louisville Slugger produced for the big leagues were made from maple.

HOME SWEET HOME

The Louisville Slugger brand was back in its groove, but it was not in its original location. Still based across the river from Louisville in Indiana, Jack Hillerich recognized his company needed to reclaim its heritage and get out of its now-oversized manufacturing facility. With annual wooden bat production diminished to just 1 million, Hillerich & Bradsby did not need the 25 lathes at the factory in Slugger Park. Besides, many still felt Louisville Slugger belonged in Louisville where the Hillerich family founded the brand more than a century before. City of Louisville leaders agreed, working to woo the company back across the river.

Dialogue began when the mayor paid a visit to Hillerich, seeing if he was interested in providing a hand lathe for a storefront display on Main Street. Hillerich responded by saying he wanted to

put his whole factory back in Louisville. A community council of business and baseball people was pulled together. Ultimately it recommended a new site on the river, near the Kennedy Bridge. A concept was discussed and called for a 200-foot tall Louisville Slugger bat replica with an elevator inside that would serve as a welcome to Louisville the way the Arch serves St. Louis, Missouri. The site was buffered by a junkyard, however, and Hillerich could not see building a new factory next to a junkyard.

After a four-year search, he finally settled on a site at downtown Louisville's Eighth and Main Streets. The location was not only near the factory his grandfather and great-grandfather had started in the 1880s; it also shared architectural similarities,

Jack Hillerich and Louisville mayor Jerry Abramson worked together on bringing Hillerich & Bradsby back to its hometown.

127

Derek Jeter

New York Yankees captain Derek Jeter has what many consider a dream job. Playing shortstop for one of the most recognized franchises in all of professional sports, Jeter is one of the highest-paid players in professional baseball. He won the AL Rookie of the Year Award his first season with the Yankees, has since been named to the All-Star team nine times, and led New York to four World Series championships while maintaining a .316 career batting average. Jeter says, however, that he began playing baseball only because he wanted to emulate his father.

"I wanted to be like him," said Jeter.

His father had been a shortstop at Fisk University in Tennessee. When Derek began playing organized baseball in Michigan at the age of six, he remembers wanting to move the way his father moved when they played catch.

Following an outstanding career at Kalamazoo's Central High School which earned Jeter two prominent national player of the year awards following his senior season, he signed a baseball scholarship with Michigan but opted in 1992 to sign with the Yankees, his favorite childhood team, after the franchise made him the sixth-overall choice in the draft.

Derek Jeter's grandmother was a Yankees fan, but she probably never dared to imagine that her quiet young grandson would one day grab a 34-inch, 32-ounce P72 ash Louisville Slugger and help lead her precious Yankees back to the upper echelon of Major League Baseball. After four years in the minor leagues, Jeter debuted with the Yankees in 1995 and was the team's starting shortstop on Opening Day in 1996. He has been one of the best and most consistent hitters in baseball ever since, amassing more than 2,500 hits thus far and winning three Silver Slugger Awards (2006, 2007, and 2008). In his rookie year, he began his legendary postseason career by hitting .361 to help the team win its first World Series championship since 1978.

Although Jeter and teammates missed the World Series the next year, they came back for three World Series championships in a row in 1998, 1999, and 2000—and Jeter's bat and glove were critical in each one. He hit .324 in 1998 and a career-high .349 in 1999. Not finished yet, Jeter went on the next year to capture not only the MVP awards for the All-Star Game and the World Series, but the Yankees also took home the fourth championship in his first five years in the majors.

At times, Jeter's swing is so smooth he makes hitting in the big leagues look easy, but Jeter is quick to argue nothing could be further from the truth.

"People have said before that hitting a baseball is the toughest thing to do in professional sports," said Jeter. "It is hand-eye coordination, and you have such little time to decide whether you are going to swing or not that you have to be prepared to swing on every pitch. You just anticipate that on every pitch you are going to try and make contact.

"You put a lot of work in at batting practice, hitting off a tee, taking soft toss, taking extra batting practice. Then when you get in the game, that's when you are supposed to have a good time and you are supposed to let your ability take over."

"I go up there and basically I don't guess pitches. I just try to see the ball and hit it," Jeter once said on camera for a Louisville Slugger video.

When that one good pitch comes, Jeter hopes to make it count. If everything comes together properly, he does not even feel the bat crack the ball.

"You don't really feel it," said Jeter. "Once you have made contact, you do not feel yourself hitting the ball. It is like you are swinging and you hit the ball so well that it is like you are swinging through nothing. That's one of those things you wish could happen a little bit more often than it does."

In 2003, he became only the 11th player in history to be named a Captain of the Yankees.

"I think maybe, in each at-bat, if you're lucky you might get one good pitch to hit, and if you miss it then you're in trouble."

—DEREK JETER

Derek Jeter is a nine-time All-Star and in 2000 won MVP awards in both the All-Star Game and the World Series.

The Louisville Slugger
Museum & Factory
attracts nearly a
quarter of a million
visitors each year.

including red brick and tall ceilings. Sterling Little, the architect of the project, adapted the original giant bat concept, settling on a plan that leaned a 120-foot tall, 68,000-pound carbon-steel replica of Babe Ruth's bat against the company's five-story headquarters. Naturally, Hillerich loved the concept. Louisville Slugger was headed home.

CREATE AN EXPERIENCE

Because baseball is a game of tradition and history, the Hillerich family wanted to make sure the return of Louisville Slugger to downtown Louisville was accompanied by the best fan and customer experience possible. Since the company's earliest days, thousands of people, from schoolchildren to baseball players, have wanted to tour Hillerich & Bradsby's manufacturing facility. After all, the sight of wooden bats made from scratch by lathe is quite uncommon, a process made infinitely more interesting upon the realization that finished bats are soon to be used by players including Derek Jeter, Lance Berkman, and Dustin Pedroia. For decades, the company obliged, letting individuals and tour groups wander through its facility while bats were being made; the company did not even charge admission, pulling employees from their desks to give visitors tour through the factory as saws whizzed and whirred around them.

When the museum concept was discussed, Jack Hillerich knew the company needed to honor its colorful past in a way that allowed fans to touch, feel, and see the history of America's pastime through the bat manufacturer's eyes. He visited some of the nation's best interactive museums, including a trip to the National Civil Rights Museum in Birmingham,

Alabama. Anchored by the signature giant replica Louisville Slugger bat leaning against the facility, Hillerich & Bradsby opened its new headquarters and the Louisville Slugger Museum & Factory tour in 1996 to rave reviews.

Drawing more than 225,000 visitors each year, the museum is a favorite daily stop for Jack Hillerich, said to be the company's best tour guide if guests are fortunate enough to bump into him. He can talk about the bat Hank Aaron used to hit his 700th home run or the bat Ty Cobb cobbled together with nails. And he is full of stories like the one about Hall of Famer Orlando Cepeda, who used to give his Louisville Slugger bat away after hitting a home run because he believed all of its power had been used up.

Among Jack Hillerich's favorite stops on the museum tour is the final stop—the factory floor. Though he tried hand-turning a bat once as his father and grandfather had done, he preferred the mechanics of the manufacturing floor and loves watching the process at work. As Marty Archer says, "The wood bat is Jack's soul."

Still in use in the factory is equipment used by Hillerich & Bradsby more than 80 years ago, including the dip line used to drop freshly sawed bats into lacquer for finishing. "My grandfather started that," Hillerich says.

The lathes have all been upgraded, save the one hand-finishing model used for visitor demonstrations. Today, two operators can run six of the automatic lathes at once, whereas years before, all one operator could manage was feeding one lathe one bat at a time. Plexiglas screens are all that shield Hillerich & Bradsby's craftsmen from

1996

A NEW HILLERICH & BRADSBY CORPORATE OFFICE, THE LOUISVILLE SLUGGER MUSEUM, AND THE BAT MANUFACTURING FACILITY OPEN AS THE COMPANY MOVES BACK TO DOWNTOWN LOUISVILLE ONTO WEST MAIN STREET

The Louisville Slugger Museum & Factory in downtown Louisville features a 120-foot-tall replica Slugger bat.

"I've got the best job in baseball.
I watch those guys use my bats,
and I get a real sense of accomplishment."

—DANNY LUCKETT

Danny Luckett remains one of the few people who can still hand-turn a bat to the exact specifications of a major league player. Today he operates computerized machinery that meets the same exacting standards of the craftsmen who began making wooden bats 125 years ago.

the viewing public as they make hundreds of bats each day, filling slots for specially ordered bats before they make their trip to the branding machine. Heated to 1,400 degrees, the machine stamps "Louisville Slugger" and the player's signature on each personalized bat. Some professional players require as many as 125 bats a year, while others get by on half as many. Regardless, a majority of the custom-made player bats are born from the hands of one man.

THE BAT MAN

Danny Luckett considers himself the luckiest man in baseball. He brushes history every single day during the Major League Baseball season. Very few people in the world can say that, he says, and

the workplace advantage is one Luckett has not grown weary after more than 38 years on the job. As the primary operator of Hillerich & Bradsby's pro player lathes since the 1970s, Luckett has made several hundred customized bats each day for the world's best players, and one of his favorite pastimes is turning on the television to see a bat he handled in action. He does not have to look hard, because the majority of Major League Baseball players swing Louisville Sluggers. When Hank Aaron hit his 700th career home run, for example, he was using a Louisville Slugger. And Joe Carter was using one when he hit a World-Series–winning home run in the bottom of the ninth inning in 1993 for the Toronto Blue Jays.

Luckett operates the company's top-line machinery, which rests near the final turn of the Louisville Slugger Factory tour. Visitors can see him in action, loading computerized instructions into the system and guiding the wood through the process, resulting in another bat headed toward the big leagues.

Even though bat-making processes have improved since the first Louisville Slugger was made 125 years ago, the basics are essentially the same. Hillerich & Bradsby places an order for wood, typically either white ash or maple. Trees, usually between 40 and 60 years old, are selected and cut into 40-inch-long sections that are then cut again into several three-inch-in-diameter billets.

Before the billets are delivered to the company, they are dried in kilns for six to eight weeks, eliminating moisture and curing the wood. At the factory, billets are stacked until ready for use. If they are big-league player bats made by Luckett on the tracer lathe—a digital machine able to cut within fractions of an inch—a metal pattern in the shape of the bat being made is placed down to prime the machine for its customized cut. Because bats come in all shapes and sizes with variations in barrel, length, weight, and handle dimensions, the company has thousands of patterns on file.

Most professional players use multiple bat models during their career, often changing during the season according to feel. At Louisville Slugger, each bat model is assigned a model number, like Babe Ruth's model No. R43, which varied from 35 to 36 inches in length and 36 to 47 ounces in weight. Bat models dating back to the company's earliest days, which include some ordered by

Danny Luckett prepares another order of big-league bats.

universities and college players in addition to handwritten order forms from professional players, are stored in the museum.

To get a true sense of how intertwined the history of Louisville Slugger and Major League Baseball really is, fans can look upon the Signature Wall in the museum, which lists each of the more than 8,500 professional players who have endorsed a version of a Louisville Slugger, customized to their liking and etched with their name. The signature from each player's autographed bat contract is used to brand a small, wooden rectangle forever displayed on the wall of the Louisville Slugger Museum & Factory.

K DENSON

"MERF" DE NUBIL

1937

Deutsch

EUTSCH

Von Derang

VINCE DE VAN

1937

Maggio

MAGGIO

Joe Di Maggio

JOE DI MAGGI

More than 8,500 player signatures adorn the Signature Wall at the Louisville Slugger Museum & Factory.

Evan Longoria
helped lead the
Tampa Bay Rays
to the 2008 World
Series.

Louisville Slugger Autographed Bat Contracts: A Sign of Great Things to Come?

When Hillerich & Bradsby signs contracts with players to have their signatures branded onto the barrel of their bats, it usually means these are players to watch. The company has a good record of picking players whose early success carries them to long-term greatness.

Consider the names of the legendary players whose names are associated with their autographed bats, including Honus Wagner, Ty Cobb, Babe Ruth, Ted Williams, Stan Musial, Joe DiMaggio, Jackie Robinson, Mickey Mantle, Roberto Clemente, Hank Aaron, Harmon Killebrew, George Brett, Kirby Puckett, Tony Gwynn, and Cal Ripken Jr., to name just a few.

Among the many current players also under contract with Louisville Slugger are Derek Jeter, Ken Griffey Jr., Manny Ramirez, Prince Fielder, and Jim Thome. Is having a signature-branded Louisville Slugger proof of greatness? There certainly are no guarantees, but consider these facts: among National Baseball Hall of Fame inductees, 80 percent had autographed Louisville Slugger bat agreements. In 2007, 13 members of the Major League Baseball All-Star team were under contract.

The historical results linking Louisville Slugger with many of the game's best players begs a natural question: what future stars have signed on, and which ones are heading for hitting greatness? In 2007, 10 players inked bat contracts with Louisville Slugger, including:

Shelley Duncan, New York Yankees
Brett Gardner, New York Yankees
Alex Gordon, Kansas City Royals
Howie Kendrick, Los Angeles Angels of Anaheim
Evan Longoria, Tampa Bay Rays
Dustin Pedroia, Boston Red Sox
Juan Pierre, Los Angeles Dodgers
Colby Rasmus, St. Louis Cardinals
Ryan Spilborghs, Colorado Rockies
Troy Tulowitzki, Colorado Rockies

If history is any indicator, several of the players on this list will emerge as hitting stars, but three have already shown themselves worthy of someday being mentioned in the same breath as the game's greats.

Third baseman Evan Longoria, whose Rays surprisingly reached the 2008 World Series, uses the same I13 model Louisville Slugger as Tulowitzski, including the same length and weight, but in ash wood and with a heavy flame treatment. In his rookie season, Longoria hit .272 with 27 home runs, and his .531 slugging percentage placed him an impressive eighth in the American League. He also started in the All-Star Game and took home the AL Rookie of the Year Award.

Dustin Pedroia has already notched a number of milestones, including winning the 2007 AL Rookie of the Year and the 2008 AL MVP Award. In 2007, his .317 batting average was 10th overall and helped his Red Sox win the World Series. In 2008, he led the American League in hits (213), doubles (54), and runs (118), and his .326 batting average was second in the league. Pedroia swings a black-finished, maple S318 cupped Louisville Slugger, which is 33.5 inches long and weighs 30.5 ounces.

Rockies shortstop Troy Tulowitzki debuted in the majors in 2006. Swinging a 33.5-inch, 31.5-ounce, I13 maple bat with a black finish, he hit 24 home runs in 2007—third among all rookies that year. His career batting average is .276, with 33 home runs and 151 RBIs.

Dustin Pedroia won the AL MVP Award in 2008.

In 2007, Troy Tulowitzki led NL rookies in at-bats, hits, and RBIs.

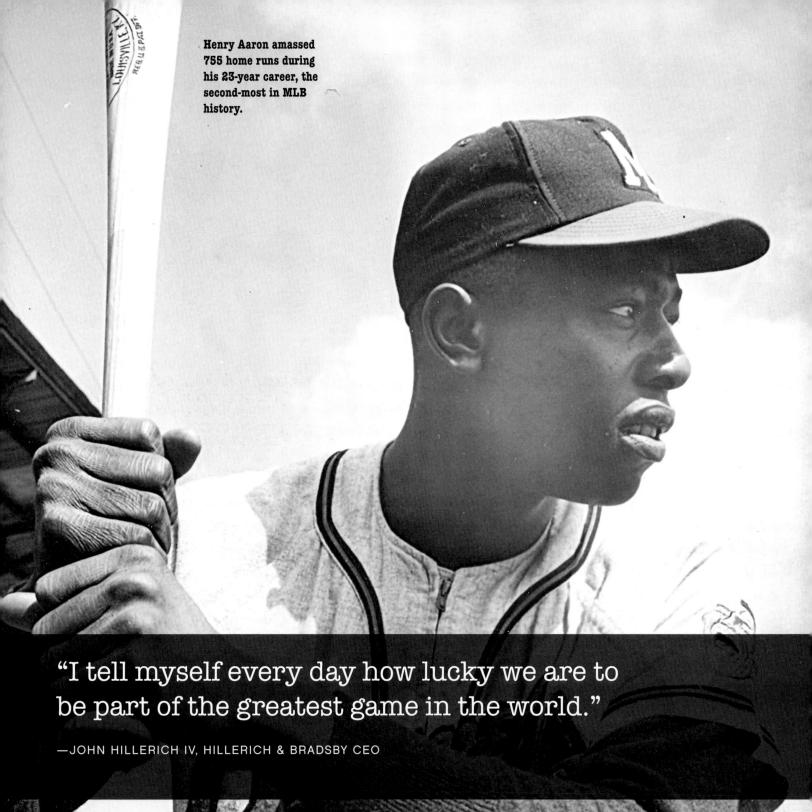

Henry Aaron amassed 755 home runs during his 23-year career, the second-most in MLB history.

"I tell myself every day how lucky we are to be part of the greatest game in the world."

—JOHN HILLERICH IV, HILLERICH & BRADSBY CEO

8

Celebrating a Milestone

On a warm summer day, when 30 Major League Baseball teams and thousands of youth teams are preparing to play games across America, with half or more of all those players likely wielding a favorite Louisville Slugger bat, John Hillerich IV can only sit back and marvel at how far the Hillerich family tradition and Louisville Slugger baseball legacy has come.

Named company CEO in 2001 when his father, Jack Hillerich, retired as Hillerich & Bradsby's day-to-day leader to assume a chairmanship role, John Hillerich understood from the day he took over the burden he has to bear in leading a business that is not only linked to family tradition, but also intricately woven into American history. As the company nears its 125th anniversary, John Hillerich talks about the bat's achievement in baseball, beginning with Pete Browning in 1884 and continuing with the Tampa Bay Rays' Evan Longoria, the 2008 AL Rookie of the Year.

During a history marked by fire, flood, generational leadership change, and the evolution of the game, Hillerich & Bradsby and its famed Louisville Slugger bat has managed to not only survive one-quarter into its second century of business but thrive. The company still caters to both the best players in baseball as well as the thousands of young players who stand in at the plate, game after game, hoping to make a memory every time a pitch enters into the strike zone.

2001

JOHN HILLERICH
IV SUCCEEDS HIS
FATHER AS CEO
AND PRESIDENT,
BECOMING THE FIFTH
GENERATION OF
HILLERICHS TO LEAD
THE COMPANY; JACK
HILLERICH REMAINS
AS CHAIRMAN OF
THE BOARD

**John A. Hillerich IV
became CEO of Hillerich
& Bradsby in 2001.**

Some hitters, such as Ty Cobb, Joe DiMaggio, and Pete Rose, collected thousands of hits with Louisville Slugger bats. Others may have earned only a handful before moving on from baseball at an early age to pursue other goals. All, however, have shared the same unique connection to baseball's legacy as the Hillerich family and the employees who have crafted the bats over the years, says John Hillerich. A bat may be a bat, after all, but there is only one Louisville Slugger; the bat was so beloved by former Yankees star Mickey Mantle that he was easily convinced by Hillerich & Bradsby to write down batting tips for publication in a company newsletter titled *The Art of Batting.*

> "You flash back to Lou Gehrig's speech or Babe Ruth stories or images of Hank Aaron circling the bases again and again, and you realize we are connected to those flashes."
>
> —JOHN HILLERICH IV

As the fifth-generation Hillerich speaks, he is reminded that his teenage son is now working for the company just one floor below. Managing a booth in the museum as a summer job, blond-haired, starry-eyed 14-year-old John Hillerich V is just steps away from Hillerich & Bradsby's model-bat filing room, where stacks of special-order templates dating back more than a century were handled by his great-great-grandfather. The sixth-generation Hillerich received a solid dose of family and baseball history during his summer employment, learning from thousands of visitors that Louisville Slugger is not just a sporting goods brand, nor is it just a family business.

"He said, 'Dad, do you know how cool this place is?'" John Hillerich IV recalls his son saying one afternoon. "He leaves for work and cannot wait to get back. He came to a realization that this is something special that is much bigger than all of us."

To continue the legacy, Hillerich & Bradsby scheduled a complete update to its popular museum for 2009. Among planned additions is one of three authentic bats, never publicly displayed before, that Joe DiMaggio used during his 56-game hitting streak in 1941, as well as an expanded exhibit and storyline for Babe Ruth's famous notched bat. Visitors will also be able to

Joe DiMaggio was one in a long line of Yankees who were proud to see their name on a Louisville Slugger.

visit "Grandpa Bud's Attic," viewing historic contracts signed by Major League Baseball greats, unique photographs, and other rare memorabilia.

"I feel the same way about it all as visitors do," says Hillerich. "We are just here as caretakers. You see that famous picture of Ted Williams kissing his bat and you get a sense of who you are and who we are. You realize what he meant to my family, to this business, and to this country."

Hillerich enjoys tracing his and Louisville Slugger's heritage along the same lines, understanding they are one and the same. The company and the brand are successful after 125 years because of the hard work of many, he says, but he also realizes it might have ended at several points along the way. Among the more treacherous times occurred in the very beginning, when his great-great-grandfather gave his son Bud Hillerich grief about spending too much time around baseball and other vices, viewing the sport as foolish and a waste of time along the lines of drinking, gambling, and womanizing.

2007

BARRY BONDS
BREAKS HANK
AARON'S HOME-
RUN RECORD WITH
762 HOMERS

Pop Culture Icon: More Than Just a Bat

Sometimes you're the windshield
Sometimes you're the bug
Sometimes it all comes together baby
Sometimes you're just a fool in love
Sometimes you're the Louisville Slugger
Sometimes you're the ball
Sometimes it all comes together
Sometimes you're gonna lose it all

From "The Bug," written by Mark Knopfler. It originally appeared on Dire Straits' *On Every Street* (1991) and has been covered by Mary Chapin Carpenter (1992), The Alex Bollard Assembly (1996), and Mike Berry & the Outlaws (2002).

Americans love brands. The brands we find irresistible become a part of our lives, even helping to define who we are to our friends and the world at large. Often those brands are accompanied by bigger-than-life icons that represent both the brand and something larger. Google isn't just an Internet company—it's now a verb and an activity. Similarly, a Louisville Slugger bat isn't just a bat—it's a connection to the past that shows up repeatedly throughout our popular culture. The famous name has come to mean more than a smooth, round stick used to hit a ball; it has become an element of our language and culture. Because of the rich tradition of players including Babe Ruth, Ted Williams, Mickey Mantle, Roger Maris, Derek Jeter, and Prince Fielder, a Slugger in anyone's hands has become a symbol of power.

One young woman in Louisville has the Louisville Slugger logo tattooed on her right bicep. "Lots of guys have it," the restaurant hostess and cosmetic consultant says. "But I'm the only girl I know of." To her, it's a symbol of local pride—and the power of her right arm.

When Mary Chapin Carpenter sang "Sometimes you're the Louisville Slugger" in 1992, no one, male or female, had to ask what she meant. More recently, Louisville Slugger played a key role in *American Idol* contestant–turned–country music star Carrie Underwood's first album, *Some Hearts*, released in August 2006. The music video for her song "Before He Cheats," which debuted at No. 1 on the charts, features Underwood walking through a parking lot with a Louisville Slugger, which she has used to smash the headlights of her boyfriend's car.

As she sings, "I took a Louisville Slugger to both headlights," few seem to question her choice of a Slugger as an authoritative weapon, as the song has been downloaded 2.5 million times (the largest number ever for a country song) and has sold more than 1 million telephone ringtones.

The name Louisville Slugger has crossed over into other art forms as well. In 2008, Gillette used Louisville Slugger bats for a television commercial featuring Derek Jeter and Tiger Woods. The set decorator was quoted as saying, "It's not a bat unless it's a Louisville Slugger." Slugger bats and gear are often requested and appear in movies and on television, including such films as *Bull Durham*, *Field of Dreams*, *Bad News Bears*, and *Benchwarmers* and the TV shows *Las Vegas* and *CSI*. When Kentucky governor Ernie Fletcher appeared on *The Tonight Show*, he presented Jay Leno with a Leno-autographed model.

A love of memorabilia and the movies led baseball fan Abel Sanchez to launch Reel Bats, a company dedicated to offering collectors limited-edition bats featuring classic baseball movies. Working with Louisville Slugger, Major League Baseball, and various movie companies, Reel Bats has begun producing collectibles such as the *Bull Durham* series of bats, featuring the "signatures" of fictional characters Crash Davis, Nuke LaLoosh, and Annie Savoy.

Louisville Slugger has also become a nickname for the F4 Phantom, a fighter-bomber perhaps best known for service during the cold war and for downing significant numbers of Soviet MiGs in various conflicts over nearly four decades of service.

The Louisville Slugger Museum & Factory in downtown Louisville is a frequent host of celebrities and political figures, including Muhammad Ali, Ken Norton, Geena Davis, Jerry Seinfeld, and members of the Dave Matthews Band, as well as President George H.W. Bush, President Bill Clinton, and President George W. Bush.

Like so many brands, the Louisville Slugger has become almost synonymous with the product category. Rick Redman, vice president of corporate communications for Hillerich & Bradsby, says that hardly a day goes by that his media monitoring reports don't show a story of someone across the U.S. defending his or her home with a baseball bat. "Whether or not it really was a Louisville Slugger, we don't always know. But in most people's minds, a baseball bat is a Louisville Slugger," he said.

The oval Louisville Slugger logo has become one of the most recognized icons in American popular culture.
Photo courtesy of Philip Shirley

2009

HILLERICH & BRADSBY
CELEBRATES THE
125TH ANNIVERSARY
OF THE FIRST
LOUISVILLE SLUGGER
BAT

When Bud Hillerich's father sold him out of the business, the Louisville Slugger brand, the family legacy—everything—could have ended almost before it began. Fortunately for baseball and the Hillerich family, it did not. Frank Bradsby knew back in 1910 he needed Bud Hillerich to remain part of the business; that turning point has been a point of protection ever since, preserving family and baseball tradition into the new millennium.

John Hillerich gives pause to wonder what Bud Hillerich might think at the company's 125th anniversary, with three generations of Hillerich family members working at Hillerich & Bradsby on the same summer day. Still the most popular bat in professional baseball and now arguably the premier bat in the college baseball game—with TPX being a part of more national championships than any other—Louisville Slugger has come a long way since the first bat was hand-turned in the 19th century. More than 100 million bats and an untold number of hits by players young and old later, Bud Hillerich's passion for serving the player is still firmly intact.

"He would probably be amazed at how much remains the same," says John Hillerich. "Everything we do relates to how it all started. Baseball is about tradition, and so is bat-making. We have never wanted to let go of that string that runs through time, tying it all together."

Although the Louisville Slugger bat has seen the most action on the baseball diamond, it has also been involved in several stories from America's military history.

During World War II, some sporting goods found their way to a German prison camp in Upper Silesia. Dr. Carroll Witten of Louisville remembers that these articles included ice skates, some baseballs, and Louisville Slugger bats. The American prisoners of war—about 26 or 27 from Kentucky—reportedly cried when they saw that familiar trademark, a sentimental reminder of home.

Don Porter, executive director of the Amateur Softball Association, served in the Korean War. During a lull in the fighting, he and some of his buddies were playing a game of softball. They had only one ball and a Louisville Slugger. When enemy action cut short the game, everyone fled to the slit trenches. One man, however, rushed back into the open, grabbed the bat, and returned to the trench. Later, the soldier simply explained that it was the only bat they had, and the thought that it might be destroyed caused him to rush out after it.

The familiar oval logo was on the first cruise missile fired in the Persian Gulf War. The missile was painted by sailors on the U.S.S. *Louisville* nuclear attack submarine, which fired the opening shot in the conflict. Each of the sailors on board received a personalized Louisville Slugger bat when the ship was originally commissioned.

Rocky Colavito of the Tigers and the
Yankees' Mickey Mantle show off
their Louisville Sluggers.

Joe DiMaggio, wife
Dorothy, and son
Joe Jr. in 1941

"Baseball is part of America, and it is a tradition
that continues because it is such a great,
timeless game. Sure, a lot has changed,
but it is all connected."

—JOHN HILLERICH IV

Acknowledgments

The authors wish to thank Hillerich & Bradsby Co., makers of the famed Louisville Slugger brand, for completely opening the company's archives and resources for this book. From the moment we talked with CEO John A. Hillerich IV, he understood the importance of telling this story in conjunction with the company's 125th anniversary. Perhaps no product has had a more lasting impact on the game than Louisville Slugger. From Babe Ruth to Derek Jeter, the greatest players have made the greatest memories with its custom-made bats. For access to how it has happened over more than a century, we are grateful. Chairman Jack Hillerich provided us with his insight into the challenges and transitions of the company in the second half of the 20th century.

Others we wish to thank at Hillerich & Bradsby include Marty Archer, president of the Louisville Slugger division, who helped us understand that this is truly "a company that cannot be replicated"; Dan Cohen, an archivist with a sense of urgency to protect the history of the company; James Sass, for his assistance in getting to the right people and for his incredible photography; Rick Redman, for key facts and contacts; Chuck Schupp, for ideas on players who "get" Louisville Slugger; Billy Williams, for unveiling decades of the company's history; and Pam Mitchell, for juggling many calendars. Thanks to Anne Jewell, executive director of the Louisville Slugger Museum & Factory, for providing access to numerous player interviews.

At Triumph Books, editorial director Tom Bast is a baseball aficionado who holds Louisville Slugger in the highest regard. He, too, was excited about the book the moment we mentioned it. We appreciate his guiding support throughout the process. We also want to thank Triumph team members including developmental editor Adam Motin, who guided the manuscript through its production; sales director Fred Walski; and publicity director Natalie King.

Appendix I: Five Generations of Hillerich & Bradsby Management

FIRST GENERATION, 1859-1911

Johann Frederick Hillerich founded J. F. Hillerich Job Turning in 1859, the company that would one day become Hillerich & Bradsby. He focused on making bed posts, roller skids, tenpins, and butter churns, building a successful business that employed some 20 workers.

SECOND GENERATION, 1897-1946

John Andrew "Bud" Hillerich joined his father in 1880 to learn the family business. He is credited with making the company's first bat in 1884, and in 1897 the company changed its name to J.F. Hillerich & Son. Bud championed the bat business, sometimes over his father's objections, and helped make Louisville Slugger the No. 1 bat maker in the world under his leadership. He also trademarked the Louisville Slugger name, created the autographed bat concept, signed the first professional player to an endorsement agreement in 1905, and made continual improvements in the bat based on player input, including registering several bat-related patents. Bud died in 1946 at the age of 80.

Frank Bradsby joined the company in 1911 and became Bud's partner. In 1916, his name was added to the door. Bradsby brought marketing ideas and energy to the company, as well as leading the company to diversify into golf club production. The ad campaign he started in 1919 helped separate Hillerich & Bradsby from the pack and take it to the top of the industry. Bradsby passed away in 1937.

THIRD GENERATION, 1946-1969

Ward Hillerich, who took over when his father Bud died in 1946, had a short three-year career leading the business before passing away after a long-term illness. His brother, **J.A. "Junie" Hillerich Jr.**, was named president and led the company from 1949 until his death in 1969. He guided the company through the post–WWII boom years in baseball, made more difficult by recurring strikes from 1950 through the 1960s. He greatly expanded the booming golf club business in Asia and the bat business throughout North America, Latin America, and Japan.

FOURTH GENERATION, 1969-2001

John A. "Jack" Hillerich III accepted leadership of the company at the age of 28, but had a feel for the internal workings that continues to fascinate him today as chairman. He is still known for spending much of his time on the shop floor looking for process improvements. His impact on the company includes building the brand by replacing the company's name on the bats with the Louisville Slugger logo, numerous technical improvements including an automated billet-handling system, and making the decision to enter the aluminum bat industry in 1970 and operate its own manufacturing plant in 1978. He stepped down as CEO in 2001, remaining as chairman of the board.

FIFTH GENERATION, 2001–

Since 2001, **John A. Hillerich IV** has guided Hillerich & Bradsby into the new millennium, overseeing continual improvements to the ever-increasing technological advancements of the aluminum bat business as well as product expansion into the Bionic Glove category, for use in baseball, golf, and tennis. In partnership with Major League Baseball, he began the "Pink Bat" fundraising event in 2006 to benefit breast cancer research.

George Kell, winner of
the inaugural Silver Bat
Award in 1949

Appendix II: The Silver Bat Award

Each year since 1949, an official of Hillerich & Bradsby has presented the Silver Bat Award to the batting champions in both the American and National Leagues. The first recipients of the Award in 1949 were George Kell of the Detroit Tigers and Jackie Robinson of the Brooklyn Dodgers, immediately establishing this as one of the top individual awards in sports. The 34-inch Silver Bat is plated in sterling and weighs approximately 56 ounces. Each bat is engraved with the player's autograph and the statistics from his batting title.

SILVER BAT WINNERS

American League

1949: George Kell (Detroit)
1950: Billy Goodman (Boston)
1951: Ferris Fain (Philadelphia)
1952: Ferris Fain (Philadelphia)
1953: Mickey Vernon (Washington)
1954: Bobby Avila (Cleveland)
1955: Al Kaline (Detroit)
1956: Mickey Mantle (New York)
1957: Ted Williams (Boston)
1958: Ted Williams (Boston)
1959: Harvey Kuenn (Detroit)
1960: Pete Runnels (Boston)
1961: Norman Cash (Detroit)
1962: Pete Runnels (Boston)
1963: Carl Yastrzemski (Boston)
1964: Tony Oliva (Minnesota)
1965: Tony Oliva (Minnesota)
1966: Frank Robinson (Baltimore)
1967: Carl Yastrzemski (Boston)
1968: Carl Yastrzemski (Boston)
1969: Rod Carew (Minnesota)
1970: Alex Johnson (California)
1971: Tony Oliva (Minnesota)
1972: Rod Carew (Minnesota)
1973: Rod Carew (Minnesota)
1974: Rod Carew (Minnesota)
1975: Rod Carew (Minnesota)
1976: George Brett (Kansas City)
1977: Rod Carew (Minnesota)
1978: Rod Carew (Minnesota)
1979: Fred Lynn (Boston)
1980: George Brett (Kansas City)
1981: Carney Lansford (Boston)
1982: Willie Wilson (Kansas City)
1983: Wade Boggs (Boston)
1984: Don Mattingly (New York)
1985: Wade Boggs (Boston)
1986: Wade Boggs (Boston)
1987: Wade Boggs (Boston)
1988: Wade Boggs (Boston)
1989: Kirby Puckett (Minnesota)
1990: George Brett (Kansas City)
1991: Julio Franco (Texas)
1992: Edgar Martinez (Seattle)
1993: John Olerud (Toronto)
1994: Paul O'Neill (New York)
1995: Edgar Martinez (Seattle)
1996: Alex Rodriguez (Seattle)
1997: Frank Thomas (Chicago)
1998: Bernie Williams (New York)
1999: Nomar Garciaparra (Boston)
2000: Nomar Garciaparra (Boston)
2001: Ichiro Suzuki (Seattle)
2002: Manny Ramirez (Boston)
2003: Bill Mueller (Boston)
2004: Ichiro Suzuki (Seattle)
2005: Michael Young (Texas)
2006: Joe Mauer (Minnesota)
2007: Magglio Ordonez (Detroit)
2008: Joe Mauer (Minnesota)

Al Kaline, Silver Bat Award winner in 1955

Rod Carew, Silver
Bat Award winner
in 1969, 1972,
1973, 1974, 1975,
1977, and 1978

National League

1949: Jackie Robinson (Brooklyn)	1979: Keith Hernandez (St. Louis)
1950: Stan Musial (St. Louis)	1980: Bill Buckner (Chicago)
1951: Stan Musial (St. Louis)	1981: Bill Madlock (Pittsburgh)
1952: Stan Musial (St. Louis)	1982: Al Oliver (Montreal)
1953: Carl Furillo (Brooklyn)	1983: Bill Madlock (Pittsburgh)
1954: Willie Mays (New York)	1984: Tony Gwynn (San Diego)
1955: Richie Ashburn (Philadelphia)	1985: Willie McGee (St. Louis)
1956: Henry Aaron (Milwaukee)	1986: Tim Raines (Montreal)
1957: Stan Musial (St. Louis)	1987: Tony Gwynn (San Diego)
1958: Richie Ashburn (Philadelphia)	1988: Tony Gwynn (San Diego)
1959: Henry Aaron (Milwaukee)	1989: Tony Gwynn (San Diego)
1960: Dick Groat (Pittsburgh)	1990: Willie McGee (St. Louis)
1961: Roberto Clemente (Pittsburgh)	1991: Terry Pendleton (Atlanta)
1962: Tommy Davis (Los Angeles)	1992: Gary Sheffield (San Diego)
1963: Tommy Davis (Los Angeles)	1993: Andres Galarraga (Colorado)
1964: Roberto Clemente (Pittsburgh)	1994: Tony Gwynn (San Diego)
1965: Roberto Clemente (Pittsburgh)	1995: Tony Gwynn (San Diego)
1966: Matty Alou (Pittsburgh)	1996: Tony Gwynn (San Diego)
1967: Roberto Clemente (Pittsburgh)	1997: Tony Gwynn (San Diego)
1968: Pete Rose (Cincinnati)	1998: Larry Walker (Colorado)
1969: Pete Rose (Cincinnati)	1999: Larry Walker (Colorado)
1970: Rico Carty (Atlanta)	2000: Todd Helton (Colorado)
1971: Joe Torre (St. Louis)	2001: Larry Walker (Colorado)
1972: Billy Williams (Chicago)	2002: Barry Bonds (San Francisco)
1973: Pete Rose (Cincinnati)	2003: Albert Pujols (St. Louis)
1974: Ralph Garr (Atlanta)	2004: Barry Bonds (San Francisco)
1975: Bill Madlock (Chicago)	2005: Derrek Lee (Chicago)
1976: Bill Madlock (Chicago)	2006: Freddy Sanchez (Pittsburgh)
1977: Dave Parker (Pittsburgh)	2007: Matt Holliday (Colorado)
1978: Dave Parker (Pittsburgh)	2008: Chipper Jones (Atlanta)

Stan Musial, Silver Bat
Award winner in 1950,
1951, 1952, and 1957

Henry Aaron, Silver Bat Award winner in 1956 and 1959

Appendix III: The Silver Slugger Award

In 1980, Hillerich & Bradsby instituted the Silver Slugger Award to recognize a "team" composed of the best offensive producers at each position in both the American and National Leagues, as voted by Major League Baseball managers and coaches. The trophy stands three feet tall and bears the engraved name of the winner and his Silver Slugger teammates in his respective league. Players are selected based on offensive statistics including batting average, on-base percentage, and slugging percentage, as well as the coaches' and managers' general impressions of a player's overall offensive value. Managers and coaches are not allowed to vote for players on their own team.

SILVER SLUGGER TEAMS

1980

American League

1B: Cecil Cooper, Milwaukee
2B: Willie Randolph, New York
3B: George Brett, Kansas City
SS: Robin Yount, Milwaukee
OF: Ben Oglivie, Milwaukee
OF: Al Oliver, Texas
OF: Willie Wilson, Kansas City
C: Lance Parrish, Detroit
DH: Reggie Jackson, New York

National League

1B: Keith Hernandez, St. Louis
2B: Manny Trillo, Philadelphia
3B : Mike Schmidt, Philadelphia
SS: Garry Templeton, St. Louis
OF: Dusty Baker, Los Angeles
OF: Andre Dawson, Montreal
OF: George Hendrick, St. Louis
C: Ted Simmons, St. Louis
P: Bob Forsch, St. Louis

1981

American League

1B: Cecil Cooper, Milwaukee
2B: Bobby Grich, California
3B: Carney Lansford, Boston
SS: Rick Burleson, California
OF: Rickey Henderson, Oakland
OF: Dave Winfield, New York
OF: Dwight Evans, Boston
C: Carlton Fisk, Chicago
DH: Al Oliver, Texas

National League

1B: Pete Rose, Philadelphia
2B: Manny Trillo, Philadelphia
3B: Mike Schmidt, Philadelphia
SS: Dave Concepcion, Cincinnati
OF: Andre Dawson, Montreal
OF: George Foster, Cincinnati
OF: Dusty Baker, Los Angeles
C: Gary Carter, Montreal
P: Fernando Valenzuela, Los Angeles

1982

American League

1B: Cecil Cooper, Milwaukee
2B: Damaso Garcia, Toronto
3B: Doug DeCinces, California
SS: Robin Yount, Milwaukee
OF: Dave Winfield, New York
OF: Willie Wilson, Kansas City
OF: Reggie Jackson, California
C: Lance Parrish, Detroit
DH: Hal McRae, Kansas City

National League

1B: Al Oliver, Montreal
2B: Joe Morgan, San Francisco
3B: Mike Schmidt, Philadelphia
SS: Dave Concepcion, Cincinnati
OF: Dale Murphy, Atlanta
OF: Pedro Guerrero, Los Angeles
OF: Leon Durham, Chicago
C: Gary Carter, Montreal
P: Don Robinson, Pittsburgh

1983
American League
> 1B: Eddie Murray, Baltimore
> 2B: Lou Whitaker, Detroit
> 3B: Wade Boggs, Boston
> SS: Cal Ripken Jr., Baltimore
> OF: Jim Rice, Boston
> OF: Dave Winfield, New York
> OF: Lloyd Moseby, Toronto
> C: Lance Parrish, Detroit
> DH: Don Baylor, New York

National League
> 1B: George Hendrick, St. Louis
> 2B: Johnny Ray, Pittsburgh
> 3B: Mike Schmidt, Philadelphia
> SS: Dickie Thon, Houston
> OF: Andre Dawson, Montreal
> OF: Dale Murphy, Atlanta
> OF: Jose Cruz, Houston
> C: Terry Kennedy, San Diego
> P: Fernando Valenzuela, Los Angeles

1984
American League
> 1B: Eddie Murray, Baltimore
> 2B: Lou Whitaker, Detroit
> 3B: Buddy Bell, Texas
> SS: Cal Ripken Jr., Baltimore
> OF: Tony Armas, Boston
> OF: Jim Rice, Boston
> OF: Dave Winfield, New York
> C: Lance Parrish, Detroit
> DH: Andre Thornton, Cleveland

National League
> 1B: Keith Hernandez, New York
> 2B: Ryne Sandberg, Chicago
> 3B: Mike Schmidt, Philadelphia
> SS: Garry Templeton, San Diego
> OF: Dale Murphy, Atlanta
> OF: Jose Cruz, Houston
> OF: Tony Gwynn, San Diego
> C: Gary Carter, Montreal
> P: Rick Rhoden, Pittsburgh

Sweet Spot

1985

American League

    1B: Don Mattingly, New York
    2B: Lou Whitaker, Detroit
    3B: George Brett, Kansas City
    SS: Cal Ripken Jr., Baltimore
    OF: Rickey Henderson, New York
    OF: Dave Winfield, New York
    OF: George Bell, Toronto
    C: Carlton Fisk, Chicago
    DH: Don Baylor, New York

National League

    1B: Jack Clark, St. Louis
    2B: Ryne Sandberg, Chicago
    3B: Tim Wallach, Montreal
    SS: Hubie Brooks, Montreal
    OF: Willie McGee, St. Louis
    OF: Dale Murphy, Atlanta
    OF: Dave Parker, Cincinnati
    C: Gary Carter, New York
    P: Rick Rhoden, Pittsburgh

1986

American League

    1B: Don Mattingly, New York
    2B: Frank White, Kansas City
    3B: Wade Boggs, Boston
    SS: Cal Ripken Jr., Baltimore
    OF: George Bell, Toronto
    OF: Kirby Puckett, Minnesota
    OF: Jesse Barfield, Toronto
    C: Lance Parrish, Detroit
    DH: Don Baylor, Boston

National League

    1B: Glenn Davis, Houston
    2B: Steve Sax, Los Angeles
    3B: Mike Schmidt, Philadelphia
    SS: Hubie Brooks, Montreal
    OF: Tony Gwynn, San Diego
    OF: Tim Raines, Montreal
    OF: Dave Parker, Cincinnati
    C: Gary Carter, New York
    P: Rick Rhoden, Pittsburgh

1987

American League

    1B: Don Mattingly, New York
    2B: Lou Whitaker, Detroit
    3B: Wade Boggs, Boston
    SS: Alan Trammell, Detroit
    OF: George Bell, Toronto
    OF: Dwight Evans, Boston
    OF: Kirby Puckett, Minnesota
    C: Matt Nokes, Detroit
    DH: Paul Molitor, Milwaukee

National League

    1B: Jack Clark, St. Louis
    2B: Juan Samuel, Philadelphia
    3B: Tim Wallach, Montreal
    SS: Ozzie Smith, St. Louis
    OF: Andre Dawson, Chicago
    OF: Eric Davis, Cincinnati
    OF: Tony Gwynn, San Diego
    C: Benito Santiago, San Diego
    P: Bob Forsch, St. Louis

1988

American League

    1B: George Brett, Kansas City
    2B: Julio Franco, Cleveland
    3B: Wade Boggs, Boston
    SS: Alan Trammell, Detroit
    OF: Kirby Puckett, Minnesota
    OF: Jose Canseco, Oakland
    OF: Mike Greenwell, Boston
    C: Carlton Fisk, Chicago
    DH: Paul Molitor, Milwaukee

National League

    1B: Andres Galarraga, Montreal
    2B: Ryne Sandberg, Chicago
    3B: Bobby Bonilla, Pittsburgh
    SS: Barry Larkin, Cincinnati
    OF: Darryl Strawberry, New York
    OF: Andy Van Slyke, Pittsburgh
    OF: Kirk Gibson, Los Angeles
    C: Benito Santiago, San Diego
    P: Tim Leary, Los Angeles

1989

American League

    1B: Fred McGriff, Toronto
    2B: Julio Franco, Texas
    3B: Wade Boggs, Boston
    SS: Cal Ripken Jr., Baltimore
    OF: Kirby Puckett, Minnesota
    OF: Ruben Sierra, Texas
    OF: Robin Yount, Milwaukee
    C: Mickey Tettleton, Baltimore
    DH: Harold Baines, Chicago/Texas

National League

    1B: Will Clark, San Francisco
    2B: Ryne Sandberg, Chicago
    3B: Howard Johnson, New York
    SS: Barry Larkin, Cincinnati
    OF: Kevin Mitchell, San Francisco
    OF: Tony Gwynn, San Diego
    OF: Eric Davis, Cincinnati
    C: Craig Biggio, Houston
    P: Don Robinson, San Francisco

1990

American League

    1B: Cecil Fielder, Detroit
    2B: Julio Franco, Texas
    3B: Kelly Gruber, Toronto
    SS: Alan Trammell, Detroit
    OF: Rickey Henderson, Oakland
    OF: Jose Canseco, Oakland
    OF: Ellis Burks, Boston
    C: Lance Parrish, California
    DH: Dave Parker, Milwaukee

National League

    1B: Eddie Murray, Los Angeles
    2B: Ryne Sandberg, Chicago
    3B: Matt Williams, San Francisco
    SS: Barry Larkin, Cincinnati
    OF: Barry Bonds, Pittsburgh
    OF: Bobby Bonilla, Pittsburgh
    OF: Darryl Strawberry, New York
    C: Benito Santiago, San Diego
    P: Don Robinson, San Francisco

1991

American League

    1B: Cecil Fielder, Detroit
    2B: Julio Franco, Texas
    3B: Wade Boggs, Boston
    SS: Cal Ripken Jr., Baltimore
    OF: Jose Canseco, Oakland
    OF: Joe Carter, Toronto
    OF: Ken Griffey Jr., Seattle
    C: Mickey Tettleton, Detroit
    DH: Frank Thomas, Chicago

National League

    1B: Will Clark, San Francisco
    2B: Ryne Sandberg, Chicago
    3B: Howard Johnson, New York
    SS: Barry Larkin, Cincinnati
    OF: Barry Bonds, Pittsburgh
    OF: Bobby Bonilla, Pittsburgh
    OF: Ron Gant, Atlanta
    C: Benito Santiago, San Diego
    P: Tom Glavine, Atlanta

1992

American League

    1B: Mark McGwire, Oakland
    2B: Roberto Alomar, Toronto
    3B: Edgar Martinez, Seattle
    SS: Travis Fryman, Detroit
    OF: Joe Carter, Toronto
    OF: Juan Gonzalez, Texas
    OF: Kirby Puckett, Minnesota
    C: Mickey Tettleton, Detroit
    DH: Dave Winfield, Toronto

National League

    1B: Fred McGriff, San Diego
    2B: Ryne Sandberg, Chicago
    3B: Gary Sheffield, San Diego
    SS: Barry Larkin, Cincinnati
    OF: Barry Bonds, Pittsburgh
    OF: Andy Van Slyke, Pittsburgh
    OF: Larry Walker, Montreal
    C: Darren Daulton, Philadelphia
    P: Dwight Gooden, New York

1993

American League

    1B: Frank Thomas, Chicago
    2B: Carlos Baerga, Cleveland
    3B: Wade Boggs, New York
    SS: Cal Ripken Jr., Baltimore
    OF: Albert Belle, Cleveland
    OF: Juan Gonzalez, Texas
    OF: Ken Griffey Jr., Seattle
    C: Mike Stanley, New York
    DH: Paul Molitor, Toronto

National League

    1B: Fred McGriff, San Diego/Atlanta
    2B: Robby Thompson, San Francisco
    3B: Matt Williams, San Francisco
    SS: Jay Bell, Pittsburgh
    OF: Barry Bonds, San Francisco
    OF: Lenny Dykstra, Philadelphia
    OF: David Justice, Atlanta
    C: Mike Piazza, Los Angeles
    P: Orel Hershiser, Los Angeles

1994

American League

    1B: Frank Thomas, Chicago
    2B: Carlos Baerga, Cleveland
    3B: Wade Boggs, New York
    SS: Cal Ripken Jr., Baltimore
    OF: Albert Belle, Cleveland
    OF: Ken Griffey Jr., Seattle
    OF: Kirby Puckett, Minnesota
    C: Ivan Rodriguez, Texas
    DH: Julio Franco, Chicago

National League

    1B: Jeff Bagwell, Houston
    2B: Craig Biggio, Houston
    3B: Matt Williams, San Francisco
    SS: Wil Cordero, Montreal
    OF: Moises Alou, Montreal
    OF: Barry Bonds, San Francisco
    OF: Tony Gwynn, San Diego
    C: Mike Piazza, Los Angeles
    P: Mark Portugal, San Francisco

1995

American League

- 1B: Mo Vaughn, Boston
- 2B: Chuck Knoblauch, Minnesota
- 3B: Gary Gaetti, Kansas City
- SS: John Valentin, Boston
- OF: Albert Belle, Cleveland
- OF: Tim Salmon, California
- OF: Manny Ramirez, Cleveland
- C: Ivan Rodriguez, Texas
- DH: Edgar Martinez, Seattle

National League

- 1B: Eric Karros, Los Angeles
- 2B: Craig Biggio, Houston
- 3B: Vinny Castilla, Colorado
- SS: Barry Larkin, Cincinnati
- OF: Dante Bichette, Colorado
- OF: Tony Gwynn, San Diego
- OF: Sammy Sosa, Chicago
- C: Mike Piazza, Los Angeles
- P: Tom Glavine, Atlanta

1996

American League

- 1B: Mark McGwire, Oakland
- 2B: Roberto Alomar, Baltimore
- 3B: Jim Thome, Cleveland
- SS: Alex Rodriguez, Seattle
- OF: Albert Belle, Cleveland
- OF: Ken Griffey Jr., Seattle
- OF: Juan Gonzalez, Texas
- C: Ivan Rodriguez, Texas
- DH: Paul Molitor, Minnesota

National League

- 1B: Andres Galarraga, Colorado
- 2B: Eric Young, Colorado
- 3B: Ken Caminiti, San Diego
- SS: Barry Larkin, Cincinnati
- OF: Ellis Burks, Colorado
- OF: Barry Bonds, San Francisco
- OF: Gary Sheffield, Florida
- C: Mike Piazza, Los Angeles
- P: Tom Glavine, Atlanta

1997

American League

1B: Tino Martinez, New York

2B: Chuck Knoblauch, Minnesota

3B: Matt Williams, Cleveland

SS: Nomar Garciaparra, Boston

OF: David Justice, Cleveland

OF: Ken Griffey Jr., Seattle

OF: Juan Gonzalez, Texas

C: Ivan Rodriguez, Texas

DH: Edgar Martinez, Seattle

National League

1B: Jeff Bagwell, Houston

2B: Craig Biggio, Houston

3B: Vinny Castilla, Colorado

SS: Jeff Blauser, Atlanta

OF: Larry Walker, Colorado

OF: Barry Bonds, San Francisco

OF: Tony Gwynn, San Diego

C: Mike Piazza, Los Angeles

P: John Smoltz, Atlanta

1998

American League

1B: Rafael Palmeiro, Baltimore

2B: Damion Easley, Detroit

3B: Dean Palmer, Detroit

SS: Alex Rodriguez, Seattle

OF: Ken Griffey Jr., Seattle

OF: Albert Belle, Chicago

OF: Juan Gonzalez, Texas

C: Ivan Rodriguez, Texas

DH: Jose Canseco, Toronto

National League

1B: Mark McGwire, St. Louis

2B: Craig Biggio, Houston

3B: Vinny Castilla, Colorado

SS: Barry Larkin, Cincinnati

OF: Sammy Sosa, Chicago

OF: Moises Alou, Houston

OF: Greg Vaughn, San Diego

C: Mike Piazza, New York

P: Tom Glavine, Atlanta

1999

American League

1B: Carlos Delgado, Toronto

2B: Roberto Alomar, Cleveland

3B: Dean Palmer, Detroit

SS: Alex Rodriguez, Seattle

OF: Ken Griffey Jr., Seattle

OF: Manny Ramirez, Cleveland

OF: Shawn Green, Toronto

C: Ivan Rodriguez, Texas

DH: Rafael Palmeiro, Texas

National League

1B: Jeff Bagwell, Houston

2B: Edgardo Alfonzo, New York

3B: Chipper Jones, Atlanta

SS: Barry Larkin, Cincinnati

OF: Sammy Sosa, Chicago

OF: Larry Walker, Colorado

OF: Vladimir Guerrero, Montreal

C: Mike Piazza, New York

P: Mike Hampton, Houston

2000

American League

1B: Carlos Delgado, Toronto

2B: Roberto Alomar, Cleveland

3B: Troy Glaus, Anaheim

SS: Alex Rodriguez, Seattle

OF: Darin Erstad, Anaheim

OF: Manny Ramirez, Cleveland

OF: Magglio Ordonez, Chicago

C: Jorge Posada, New York

DH: Frank Thomas, Chicago

National League

1B: Todd Helton, Colorado

2B: Jeff Kent, San Francisco

3B: Chipper Jones, Atlanta

SS: Edgar Renteria, St. Louis

OF: Sammy Sosa, Chicago

OF: Barry Bonds, San Francisco

OF: Vladimir Guerrero, Montreal

C: Mike Piazza, New York

P: Mike Hampton, New York

Jorge Posada, Silver Slugger
Award winner in 2000, 2001,
2002, 2003, and 2007

2001

American League

    1B: Jason Giambi, Oakland
    2B: Bret Boone, Seattle
    3B: Troy Glaus, Anaheim
    SS: Alex Rodriguez, Texas
    OF: Juan Gonzalez, Cleveland
    OF: Manny Ramirez, Boston
    OF: Ichiro Suzuki, Seattle
    C: Jorge Posada, New York
    DH: Edgar Martinez, Seattle

National League

    1B: Todd Helton, Colorado
    2B: Jeff Kent, San Francisco
    3B: Albert Pujols, St. Louis
    SS: Rich Aurilia, San Francisco
    OF: Sammy Sosa, Chicago
    OF: Barry Bonds, San Francisco
    OF: Luis Gonzalez, Arizona
    C: Mike Piazza, New York
    P: Mike Hampton, Colorado

2002

American League

    1B: Jason Giambi, New York
    2B: Alfonso Soriano, New York
    3B: Eric Chavez, Oakland
    SS: Alex Rodriguez, Texas
    OF: Magglio Ordonez, Chicago
    OF: Bernie Williams, New York
    OF: Garret Anderson, Anaheim
    C: Jorge Posada, New York
    DH: Manny Ramirez, Boston

National League

    1B: Todd Helton, Colorado
    2B: Jeff Kent, San Francisco
    3B: Scott Rolen, St. Louis
    SS: Edgar Renteria, St. Louis
    OF: Barry Bonds, San Francisco
    OF: Sammy Sosa, Chicago
    OF: Vladimir Guerrero, Montreal
    C: Mike Piazza, New York
    P: Mike Hampton, Colorado

2003

American League

    1B: Carlos Delgado, Toronto
    2B: Bret Boone, Seattle
    3B: Bill Mueller, Boston
    SS: Alex Rodriguez, Texas
    OF: Vernon Wells, Toronto
    OF: Garret Anderson, Anaheim
    OF: Manny Ramirez, Boston
    C: Jorge Posada, New York
    DH: Edgar Martinez, Seattle

National League

    1B: Todd Helton, Colorado
    2B: Jose Vidro, Montreal
    3B: Mike Lowell, Florida
    SS: Edgar Renteria, St. Louis
    OF: Barry Bonds, San Francisco
    OF: Albert Pujols, St. Louis
    OF: Gary Sheffield, Atlanta
    C: Javy Lopez, Atlanta
    P: Mike Hampton, Atlanta

2004

American League

    1B: Mark Teixeira, Texas
    2B: Alfonso Soriano, Texas
    3B: Melvin Mora, Baltimore
    SS: Miguel Tejada, Baltimore
    OF: Manny Ramirez, Boston
    OF: Gary Sheffield, New York
    OF: Vladimir Guerrero, Anaheim
    C: (tie) Ivan Rodriguez, Detroit;
       Victor Martinez, Cleveland
    DH: David Ortiz, Boston

National League

    1B: Albert Pujols, St. Louis
    2B: Mark Loretta, San Diego
    3B: Adrian Beltre, Los Angeles
    SS: Jack Wilson, Pittsburgh
    OF: Barry Bonds, San Francisco
    OF: Jim Edmonds, St. Louis
    OF: Bobby Abreu, Philadelphia
    C: Johnny Estrada, Atlanta
    P: Livan Hernandez, Montreal

Prince Fielder, Silver
Slugger Award winner
in 2007

2005

American League

    1B: Mark Teixeira, Texas
    2B: Alfonso Soriano, Texas
    3B: Alex Rodriguez, New York
    SS: Miguel Tejada, Baltimore
    OF: Manny Ramirez, Boston
    OF: Gary Sheffield, New York
    OF: Vladimir Guerrero, Los Angeles
    C: Jason Varitek, Boston
    DH: David Ortiz, Boston

National League

    1B: Derrek Lee, Chicago
    2B: Jeff Kent, Los Angeles
    3B: Morgan Ensberg, Houston
    SS: Felipe Lopez, Cincinnati
    OF: Andruw Jones, Atlanta
    OF: Miguel Cabrera, Florida
    OF: Carlos Lee, Milwaukee
    C: Michael Barrett, Chicago
    P: Jason Marquis, St. Louis

2006

American League

    1B: Justin Morneau, Minnesota
    2B: Robinson Cano, New York
    3B: Joe Crede, Chicago
    SS: Derek Jeter, New York
    OF: Jermaine Dye, Chicago
    OF: Vladimir Guerrero, Los Angeles
    OF: Manny Ramirez, Boston
    C: Joe Mauer, Minnesota
    DH: David Ortiz, Boston

National League

    1B: Ryan Howard, Philadelphia
    2B: Chase Utley, Philadelphia
    3B: Miguel Cabrera, Florida
    SS: Jose Reyes, New York
    OF: Carlos Beltran, New York
    OF: Alfonso Soriano, Washington
    OF: Matt Holliday, Colorado
    C: Brian McCann, Atlanta
    P: Carlos Zambrano, Chicago

2007

American League

    1B: Carlos Pena, Tampa Bay
    2B: Placido Polanco, Detroit
    3B: Alex Rodriguez, New York
    SS: Derek Jeter, New York
    OF: Magglio Ordonez, Detroit
    OF: Vladimir Guerrero, Los Angeles
    OF: Ichiro Suzuki, Seattle
    C: Jorge Posada, New York
    DH: David Ortiz, Boston

National League

    1B: Prince Fielder, Milwaukee
    2B: Chase Utley, Philadelphia
    3B: David Wright, New York
    SS: Jimmy Rollins, Philadelphia
    OF: Carlos Beltran, New York
    OF: Carlos Lee, Houston
    OF: Matt Holliday, Colorado
    C: Russell Martin, Los Angeles
    P: Micah Owings, Arizona

2008

American League

    1B: Justin Morneau, Minnesota
    2B: Dustin Pedroia, Boston
    3B: Alex Rodriguez, New York
    SS: Derek Jeter, New York
    OF: Josh Hamilton, Texas
    OF: Carlos Quentin, Chicago
    OF: Grady Sizemore, Cleveland
    C: Joe Mauer, Minnesota
    DH: Aubrey Huff, Baltimore

National League

    1B: Albert Pujols, St. Louis
    2B: Chase Utley, Philadelphia
    3B: David Wright, New York
    SS: Hanley Ramirez, Florida
    OF: Matt Holliday, Colorado
    OF: Ryan Ludwick, St. Louis
    OF: Ryan Braun, Milwaukee
    C: Brian McCann, Atlanta
    P: Carlos Zambrano, Chicago

Grady Sizemore, Silver
Slugger Award winner
in 2008

Carlos Beltran and David Wright, Silver Slugger Award winners in 2007

Sources

BOOKS AND ARTICLES

Barney, Walter, editor, *A Celebration of Louisville Baseball in the Major and Minor Leagues,* Cleveland: The Society for American Baseball Research, 1997.

Hill, Bob, *Crack of the Bat: The Louisville Slugger Story,* Champaign, Illinois: Sports Publishing Inc., 2000.

Orenstein, Joshua B., "The Union Association of 1884: A Glorious Failure," *The Baseball Research Journal # 19,* 1990.

Lacer, Alan, "From Bedposts to Baseball Bats," *American Woodturner,* Summer 2007.

Montville, Leigh, *The Big Bam: The Life and Times of Babe Ruth,* New York: Doubleday, 2006.

Miller, Lori K., Lawrence W. Fielding, and Brenda G. Pitts, "The Rise of the Louisville Slugger in the Mass Market," *Sports Marketing Quarterly,* Vol. 2, Issue 3, 1993.

Musell, Bernie, "The Evolution of the Baseball Bat," Oldtyme Baseball News, Volume 4, Issue 2, Updated 1999, 2000. On file at National Baseball Hall of Fame and Museum, Inc. Research Library.

Oldham, Scott, "Louisville Slugger: The Lumber that still powers our national pastime," *Popular Mechanics,* September 1999.

Slack, Trevor, *The Commercialisation of Sport,* London: Routledge, 2004.

Stocker, Greg, *Avoiding the Corporate Death Spiral: Recognizing and Eliminating the Signs of Decline,* Milwaukee: Quality Press, 2006.

Ward, John Montgomery, *Base-Ball: How to Become a Player,* Philadelphia: The Athletic Publishing Company, 1888; reprinted in Birmingham, Alabama, by The Society for American Baseball Research, 1993, with a new foreword by Mark Alvarez.

WEBSITES

www.americaslibrary.gov
www.azlyrics.com
www.baberuth.com
www.baseball1.com
www.baseball-bats.net
www.baseballlibrary.com
www.baseball-almanac.com
www.baseball-reference.com
www.honuswagner.com
http://kclibrary.lonestar.edu
www.jewishvirtuallibrary.org
www.la84foundation.org
www.loc.gov
www.lyicsdepot.com
www.mlb.com
www.19cbaseball.com
www.nytimes.com
www.pbs.org
www.slugger.com
www.sluggermuseum.com
www.tedwilliams.com
www.tycobbmuseum.org

HILLERICH & BRADSBY ARCHIVE TRANSCRIPTS AND VIDEO

Transcripts of personal interviews and special events (some including videotape) involving Hillerich & Bradsby representatives with Major League Baseball players and coaches, including Luke Appling, Dusty Baker, Ernie Banks, Johnny Bench, George Brett, Lou Brock, Happy Chandler, Bob Feller, Steve Garvey, Tony Gwynn, Keith Hernandez, Derek Jeter, George Kell, Harmon Killebrew, Ralph Kiner, Bob Lemon, Mickey Mantle, Eddie Mathews, Johnny Mize, Stan Musial, Pee Wee Reese, Allie Reynolds, Brooks Robinson, Frank Robinson, Enos Slaughter, Andy Van Slyke, Warren Spahn, Bobby Thompson, Ted Williams, Early Wynn, and Robin Yount.

About the Authors

DAVID MAGEE is the author of 10 nonfiction books, including *Playing to Win: Jerry Jones and the Dallas Cowboys* and the acclaimed *How Toyota Became #1: Leadership Lessons from the World s Greatest Car Company*. He lives in Lookout Mountain, Tennessee, with his wife and three children. Visit his website at www.david-magee.com.

PHILIP SHIRLEY released his collection of short fiction, *Oh Don t You Cry For Me*, in 2008. He was a contributing author of *Opportunity in Adversity: How Colleges Succeed in Hard Times*, and has also been published in the acclaimed anthology *Stories from the Blue Moon Café*. His award-winning writing includes feature articles, speeches, and fiction. He is also CEO of GodwinGroup in Jackson, Mississippi.

FOR GOMMO & GOFFA—

THANK YOU FOR YOUR LOVE, STORIES, AND INSPIRATION

We are grateful to everyone who helped us with this book—we couldn't have done it without you.

Book Designer: Cheryl Meyer
Digital Artists: Per Breiehagen and Brad Palm

Text copyright © 2013 by Lori Evert
Jacket and interior photographs copyright © 2013 by Per Breiehagen

All rights reserved. Published in the United States by Random House Children's Books,
a division of Random House, Inc., New York.

Random House and the colophon are registered trademarks of Random House, Inc.

Visit us on the Web! randomhouse.com/kids
Educators and librarians, for a variety of teaching tools, visit us at RHTeachersLibrarians.com

For additional information about this book, visit TheChristmasWish.net

Library of Congress Cataloging-in-Publication Data
Evert, Lori.
The Christmas wish / by Lori Evert ; photographs by Per Breiehagen. — 1st ed.
p. cm.
Summary: Young Anja, whose greatest dream is to be one of Santa's elves, makes friends with the animals that guide her
on the journey from her home in the far North to meet Santa.
ISBN 978-0-449-81681-3 (trade) — ISBN 978-0-375-97173-0 (lib. bdg.) —
ISBN 978-0-375-98156-2 (ebook) — ISBN 978-0-449-81942-5 (read & listen ebook)
[1. Voyages and travels—Fiction. 2. Tundra animals—Fiction. 3. Santa Claus—Fiction. 4. Christmas—Fiction.
5. Arctic regions—Fiction.] I. Breiehagen, Per, ill. II. Title.
PZ7.E927Chr 2013 [Fic]—dc23 2012035529

MANUFACTURED IN CHINA   10 9 8 7 6 5 4 3 2 1   First Edition

the
CHRISTMAS
Wish

STORY BY LORI EVERT
PHOTOGRAPHS BY PER BREIEHAGEN

Random House  New York

Long, long ago, in a place so far north that the mothers never pack away the wool hats or mittens, lived a sweet little girl named Anja, whose greatest dream was to become one of Santa's Elves.

One year, as the days grew shorter and the snow had fallen for weeks without a rest, Anja decided it was time to look for Santa Claus.

Before she left, she remembered the kind old woman
who lived down the lane. She had no children or grandchildren
of her own, so Anja wanted to help her get ready for Christmas.

As the old woman napped, Anja caught her naughty cat
for her and decorated the gingerbread house they had baked
together the day before. She swept out her sauna . . .

and found a small tree for her to enjoy.

Then Anja delivered gifts to her friends and family, with a note saying she would visit them whenever her busy job with Santa would permit.

Anja was well prepared for her journey. She watched the sky at night, observing the position of the North Star, and she memorized the great map on the schoolroom wall.

*S*till, as she tied on her skis and began to glide away into the forest, Anja started to worry. "What if I get lost?" she wondered aloud.

"I can help you," sang a tiny voice.

Startled, Anja looked back to see who had spoken.

"Up here," said the voice, and a bright red bird swooped down and landed on her ski pole.

Anja explained her wish to find Santa Claus at the North Pole. "But now I wonder if I am foolish," she said.

"Not when you have the right friends," the bird answered. "If you trust me, I can help you. But we must hurry; the days are short and Christmas is very near."

So Anja skied after the patient bird, who led slowly so the child could make her way through the deep snow.

When they came to a mountainside, Anja flew so fast over the sparkling powder that the bird could barely keep up with her!

At the foot of the mountain the bird whistled, and they were greeted by a giant horse. "You may sleep in my barn tonight," he offered. "Tomorrow I can take you as far as one day and one night will allow."

The cardinal fluttered away before Anja could thank him.

Morning came in a blink. The gentle horse invited the still-sleepy Anja to climb onto his back. They talked the day away as they trod through the snowy forest.

$\mathcal{E}$vening fell as they
approached a mountain pass.
The sky came alive with
the dancing colors of the
Northern Lights. They stood
spellbound for hours and fell
asleep, the horse standing
strong and solid with Anja
lying across his warm back.

$\mathcal{A}$nja was sad when she awoke and remembered that the horse would have to leave her, but she knew that his people would be worried about him.

Later, as they approached a gleaming icefall, the horse whinnied loudly three times and from a hole in the ice appeared the oddest-looking creature Anja had ever seen.

The musk ox spoke softly and slowly. "The cardinal asked me to escort you under the glacier to the tundra," she said. Then she turned and walked back into the dark cave.

"Follow her now," the horse told Anja. "She is shy, but she is trustworthy." He saw that Anja was sad to leave him, so he said, "When you are Santa's Elf, you can visit me whenever you wish. But hurry now; Christmas is very near."

Anja took off her skis and bravely joined the plodding ox.

$\mathcal{T}$he cave was dark as night as Anja followed the ox downward, and luminescent blue as they climbed up a trail of ice and stones. When they emerged, Anja saw a tremendous fur blanket lying on the ground in front of her. Just as she was ready to collapse into its warm folds, it shifted. It rose!

It wasn't a blanket, it was an enormous bear—just like the ones in the tales her father told around the fire.

After Anja had thanked the musk ox for her help, the bear spoke. "I have come to take you north over the tundra," he said in a deep, soothing voice. "You may ski or ride as you wish, but we must hurry. Christmas is coming soon."

$\mathcal{W}$hen they stopped for a rest, Anja found a small book in her pocket. In the day's last light, she read a story to the bear about a troll and three silly little goats.

The next day was bright again. Anja skied, then rode on the bear's back. He was great company; they sang songs and made each other laugh.

They reached their destination early. Anja had no idea how the bear could tell this spot from any other, but he told her they would be meeting a friend at this exact place.

"Since we have the time, let's take another rest," he said.

Anja curled up into the bear's softness and slept without a dream.

They awoke to a jingling, jangling sound. Sleigh bells!

Anja and the bear looked up. A reindeer landed right in front of them!

"I'm so glad I found you," the reindeer said. "We must run, for I am too tired to fly."

Anja felt sorry for him; he looked exhausted. As she took his harness off, she remembered an apple she had brought and offered it to him.

The reindeer thanked her as he happily ate the apple.

Anja hugged the bear goodbye; then she put on her skis and set forth with her new friend.

At first Anja tried to ski behind the reindeer, but he was much too fast, so Anja asked him to tow her. It was as close to flying as she'd ever been.

Anja skied that way for many miles. Just as she began to worry that she could not hang on any longer, the reindeer called, "Hold tight!"

*I*n a flash, they were soaring
through the sky!

Anja watched as the ice gave
way to the ocean she had seen
on the schoolroom map. She saw
eagles, whales, and giant icebergs
that reminded her of the rock
candy she made with her mother.

Finally they landed in a lovely
clearing surrounded by trees
cloaked in snow.

Then Anja's wish came true. . . .

*S*anta Claus appeared!

He lifted Anja onto his knee. "Welcome, Anja," he said. "I have been waiting for you. You are an extraordinary little girl. While there are many children who wish to be one of Santa's Elves, you are the first to have come this far, and you are already my most important helper. You bring kindness and joy to those around you all year long. Thank you."

"Now, may I ask you for a favor?" he added with a smile. "Will you help me drive my sleigh?"

*A*nja was thrilled to give the command: "Fly!"

*I*t was very early Christmas morning when they landed near Anja's home.

"Before I leave," Santa said, "I'd like to give you a very special gift. This is a magical bell. If you ever need help, ring this bell three times."

$\mathcal{S}$anta Claus kissed her on the cheek, and the next thing she knew, she was in her bed.

Anja sat up and looked out the window and into the frosty morning. There was no sleigh, no reindeer, no tracks in the snow. She held the bell closely.

"Was it all a dream?" she wondered.

What do you think?